THE family business teeter totter

BALANCING THOSE TWO WOR(L)DS: FAMILY AND BUSINESS

Mark Wickman

© 2016 Mark Wickman

All rights reserved. No portion of this book may be reproduced, stored in a retrieval system, or transmitted in any form or by any means—electronic, mechanical, photocopy, recording, scanning, or other—except for brief quotations in critical reviews or articles, without the prior written permission of the publisher.

Published in McMinnville, Oregon, by Family Business Counsel.
www.yourfbc.com
mark.wickman@yourfbc.com

Cover design by faceoutstudio of Bend, Oregon
Interior design and typeset by Katherine Lloyd, The Desk

Some names and identifying details have been changed to protect the privacy of individuals.

ISBN: 978-0-692-74982-1

Printed in the United States of America

contents

INTRODUCTION 5

- part one -
DISCOVER

ONE	the discovery process	 13
TWO	questions	 21
THREE	conflict	 30

- part two -
IDENTIFY

FOUR	family issues	 47
FIVE	generations	 61
SIX	the roles we play and the hats we wear	 76
SEVEN	trust	 88
EIGHT	finances	 95
NINE	this thing called the business	 99

- part three -
RESOLVE

TEN	meetings	 105
ELEVEN	communication	 110
TWELVE	transitions	 120

- part four -
COMMIT

THIRTEEN	personal trainer	137
FOURTEEN	integrity	153
FIFTEEN	governance: the rules around here	162
SIXTEEN	the cultural covenant	169

- part five -
STAY ENGAGED

SEVENTEEN	changing roles	183
EIGHTEEN	the photo album	193
NINETEEN	legacy	197

ACKNOWLEDGMENTS ... 203

NOTES ... 205

introduction

I have the best job on the planet. Everything that has happened in my life so far has prepared me to do what I love to do, which is helping family businesses engage in the tough conversations that they absolutely must have but desperately try to avoid.

Part of the reason I'm here, I believe, is to help breathe hope into businesses, families, and organizations. I want them to know that achieving a strong, healthy culture is no pipe dream. Since I believe that life is meant to be lived in relationship, I remain convinced that we really can intentionally live in community.

We all want to come to a game where we can play our cards face up. We long for a fair game, where no one hides cards under the table or up their sleeve. We want to know that when we play a card someone doesn't recognize, they won't react with shock or say "Game over!" and leave.

But does such a safe place exist where we can play nice? Can we build a culture that says, "No card you play will cause me to leave the game"? I'd like to believe that kind of culture is out there. In fact, I've seen glimpses of it and I've even helped to create it, whether in family businesses or in other organizations. Over my career, I have come to believe that creating a healthy culture of communication is probably the linchpin to building a thriving business, organization, or family.

Building a Healthy Culture

When our family decided to move back to the town where I'd graduated from college, we went looking for a church. Since I still knew many people in that town, I asked a friend where we should go to church. "I think we should start one," he replied.

Over the next decade or so, many wonderful things took place in scores of lives as we wrestled with "doing church." I took some pretty strong convictions into my leadership role at the church, and together we navigated becoming a "real" church, hiring a pastor, evaluating a senior pastor's work performance, and eventually working through the departure of three senior pastors. Throughout those many years, I pondered how to most effectively manage a volunteer organization. I learned that a great deal of it has to do with building a culture of healthy communication.

During my stint in church leadership, another elder said to me, "Mark, you have a way of bringing us bad news and making us feel good about it." His comment stuck with me and became one of the reasons I do what I do today. I've learned that healthy communication takes more than pep talks and hearty slaps on the back. It also must include frank and yet helpful discussions when things go wrong or look about to go wrong.

The trouble is that all of us tend to avoid such hard but necessary conversations. Who likes conflict? Who wants to be the bad guy? Unfortunately, however, serious problems don't magically disappear simply because we wish they would. To make sure we have these necessary conversations, therefore, we all need help and encouragement. There's an art to having such talks and continuing to have them. *So* much is at stake!

What, exactly, is at stake? While you may not agree with all of the following thoughts, I suspect that at least some will resonate with you:

- *Family enterprise entails great risk.* Not only do small businesses find it difficult to survive, let alone thrive, but the very idea of *family* business carries the element of family *relationship*. What comes home with you from the office? What do you carry to the office from home? Relationships are at risk every day in a family business, and the consequences of failed relationships can be catastrophic across generations.
- *Small businesses must be run efficiently.* Large corporations can continue to exist for some time even when they don't operate efficiently. With size comes space, and with space come cracks (where "stuff" can easily fall through) and caches (size makes it easier to hide things, whether intentionally or unintentionally). Inefficient small businesses quickly go out of business.
- *Only 3 percent of family enterprises survive into the fourth generation.*[1] Why is this the case? I don't believe it's because of the economy, or because of the particular sector of the economy associated with a family business, or even because of a bad business plan. In the vast majority of cases, family enterprises fail because they never build a healthy culture of communication. Poor communication and diseased relationships kill more family businesses than anything else. One of the main reasons I do what I do is to help move that 3 percent dial.
- *Small businesses form the backbone of our communities.* Small businesses, usually family businesses, create the

jobs that provide the paychecks for families who live, shop, worship, learn, volunteer, and participate in the social fabric of our communities. But to put it bluntly, they don't get much wind put into their sails.

In *The Family Business Teeter Totter*, I want to do whatever I can to put as much wind as possible into the sails of family businesses. To do so, I will follow the general process we at Family Business Counsel use with our clients:

We developed each element in this process to help family businesses thrive, especially as they learn how to foster the kind of helpful communication that leads to success in both business and life. It works. And it will work for you too.

Has your family business taken a turn for the worse? Do you fear having some honest but necessary conversations because you worry they'll touch off a firestorm that will consume your business? Can you see trouble ahead, even though the waters appear mostly calm right now? Or does your family business seem strong and healthy, and you simply want to make sure it stays that way during a time of transition that you can see approaching on the horizon?

Wherever your business may land on the spectrum, understand that learning how to build a culture of healthy communication will provide the environment your organization needs to grow and thrive. Will your family business be one of the 3 percent that makes it into the fourth generation? It can be. May I suggest how you can make it happen? Let's move that dial!

- part one -

DISCOVER

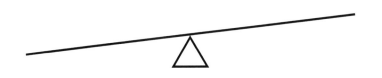

ONE

▼

the discovery process

> Over the years, I've learned that a surefooted and confident mapmaker does not a swift traveler make.
> —*Brené Brown, Daring Greatly*

I live in the Pacific Northwest, a gorgeous part of the country that frankly owes a lot to two young men who dedicated more than two years of their lives to seeing what might be out here. From May 1804 to September 1806, Meriwether Lewis and William Clark led their little band called the Corps of Discovery on an exploration of the western half of the North American continent. President Thomas Jefferson had sent them on a mission to explore and map the newly acquired Louisiana Purchase, to find a practical route from Missouri to the Pacific Ocean, to establish an American presence in the region, and to do a little scientific and economic spadework along the way.

These young explorers, both of them in their early thirties at the time, made all kinds of fascinating discoveries on their trek across the wild, uncharted frontier. They gave a young nation its first look at a part of the world it could scarcely imagine, let alone see as an integral part of the future United States of America. Their intentional focus on discovery paved the way for untold new endeavors and a sense of adventure that still hasn't died away today.

What is discovery? I like to take the word apart. It's *dis* + *covery*. It's taking off the cover and getting to the truth. It's exposing the real story so you can move forward with confidence. It's learning to face what actually is so that you can create what will be.

Discovery is where we start in working with family businesses. Always.

Even when we'd really rather start somewhere else.

It Often Doesn't Feel Good

This discovery process takes an engagement that, frankly, can feel extremely uncomfortable. Getting to the truth takes peeling away layers—layers than can make the one getting peeled feel naked and cold. Many individuals and organizations stop at just this point . . . and that's always a mistake. This discomfort, regardless of its intensity, is worth the price of admission.

Some time ago I went hiking with a couple of commercial pilots. While they didn't care what time we returned to camp, I did, because I didn't want to miss my flight. As the minutes marched on and the time approached when I had to turn back, they just kept going. I began getting angrier and angrier, fuming that they simply didn't care about my schedule. Finally, without saying a word, I turned around and headed back to the car. They kept on going.

When they rejoined me some time later, they didn't mention

my getting in a huff and leaving. They just said, "Mark, did you see the moose?"

"What moose?" I retorted.

It turned out that had I walked around just one more corner, I would have seen what they had witnessed, a majestic beast that took their breath away. But I didn't see it. Why not? Because I stopped too soon.

The process of discovery takes a commitment to persevere, even when it gets uncomfortable and even when things don't go as planned. It takes perseverance to pull off layer after layer until you uncover the gold.

Part of what makes the discovery process so uncomfortable is that through it we learn truths about *ourselves*, unpleasant truths that we'd really rather not hear spoken out loud. If discovery were all about learning the truth about someone else—if it focused on uncovering how others have screwed up and need to change—then maybe we wouldn't fear it as much as we do.

Truth is truth, however, and discovery doesn't bow to personal preferences or show partiality. To move our family businesses forward, we have to make sure they're built on truth, whether that truth concerns others or ourselves.

Do You Know Who You Are?

Chris Lowney trained for the Jesuit priesthood, left the order, went to work on Wall Street, and eventually studied to become a historian. In his great book *Heroic Leadership*, he posed the question, Why have the Jesuits survived for more than 450 years, when only 16 of the 100 largest companies in America in 1900 were even around in 2000? Lowney uncovered four unique values among the Jesuits that created a solid leadership base for the order.

The first of those unique values was *self-awareness*. The Jesuits understood their strengths, weaknesses, values, and worldview. They knew the truth about themselves, and that truth provided a strong foundation for long-term growth.[1]

How well do you know yourself? How high do you score on self-awareness?

In his book *Awareness*, Anthony de Mello declared, "It's when you're not trying that you lose things. You lose something when you're not aware."[2]

What kind of things can you lose in a family business when you remain unaware? Experience tells me that a lack of self-awareness can result in some significant losses:

- Trust
- A compelling, bright, shared vision
- A healthy culture
- Hope

If discovery is all about taking off the lid, and if a lack of awareness leads to losing things, then where are *you*? What have you lost already, or what might you lose, if you don't take off the lid and get to the truth? Could your self-awareness use some rehab?

Once I'm aware of the truth about myself, I begin to listen in a new way to you. In our work with clients, we often say, "You need to hear some things from 'Joe' that you can't hear from 'Joe.'" All of us could use a facilitator for these kinds of tough discovery conversations. We all need someone else to open up space so we can hear "Joe" differently than if we were sitting down one-on-one with him.

In our work with family businesses, we interview the team, individuals on the team, and subsets of the team. As our clients engage with one another and begin to see and feel that it's okay to take off the lid, the truth starts to come out. And as the truth comes out, a way forward often begins to take shape.

What does it take to *really* discover the truth? First, you have to find a safe place to do this. And almost always, you need someone to hold your feet to the fire. Why?

At first, this truth can seem scary and make you fearful. Through the years, however, as we've helped scores of family businesses through the discovery process, we've found that one significant by-product is often an unconditional kind of love. We've learned that the sort of truth that sets you free usually expresses itself in a way that keeps us all engaged. If we stay engaged, then we can keep talking; and if we keep talking, then eventually we'll get somewhere good.

It Takes Time

None of this happens quickly. Taking off the lid takes time. It's like the little girl who grew frustrated that she didn't get time with her daddy to tell him all about her day.

"Daddy, Daddy," she said, "let me tell you what happened today!"

Her dad, a busy and important man, replied, "Hurry up, honey. I have to get back to my work."

"But Daddy," the little girl answered, "if you want to hear about my day, you have to listen slower."

To take off the lid, all of us need to *listen slower*. This requires a different skill set than what we learned in our MBA programs. And what happens if we neglect "listening slower"? In nearly every case, we put ourselves and our organizations at great risk (as we'll see in chapter 3 when we discuss conflict).

In the book *The Innovator's Dilemma*, Clayton Christensen wrote, "The strategies and plans that managers formulate for confronting disruptive technological change ... should be plans for learning and discovery rather than plans for execution."[3] He means that we can't jump immediately to the solution. We have to take the time to discover and learn about ourselves, about others, about our situation. If we insist on getting the "execution cart" ahead of the "horse," we'll be in for a *very* unpleasant and uncomfortable journey.

At some level, all of us probably recognize the value of discovery, even if it takes time and even if it feels deeply uncomfortable. We see it played out, after all, in many arenas of life. I'll never forget one time not so long ago when I saw it play out in my own living room.

The Truth about "The Call"

Avid Seahawk fans like me were riding high after winning Super Bowl XLVIII, where we shellacked the Peyton Manning–led "unbeatable" Broncos 43–8. We continued to ride high the next year when we made it back to the Super Bowl. With a second title just a hand-off to Beast Mode away, Seattle instead handed the Lombardi trophy to the New England Patriots. And I thought, "Wait ... what just happened?"

What happened was that instead of giving the ball to Marshawn Lynch on the one-yard line, Russell Wilson threw an interception.

Game over.

"Tough loss" doesn't begin to describe the traumatizing situation for a diehard Seahawks fan like me. The call was immediately labeled the worst in NFL history. Heated discussions erupted on talk radio and on the Internet, and the Seahawks' sad story of fan angst even made its way into the national news.

Shortly after the angry cries of "Fire Bevell!" died away (Darrell Bevell is the Seahawks' offensive coordinator, responsible for calling the plays), Pete Carroll, Seattle's head coach, sat down with television personality Matt Lauer to discuss "the call." Almost six minutes into the interview, Carroll said:

> We handled the situation the way we practiced on this field right here hundreds of times. . . . I made the call that comes out of the process of the preparation and the practice . . . preparing us to do right in the situations. . . . That preparation allows me to trust in the players that they're gonna do the right thing and make the right decisions so that I never make a call thinking it's gonna go bad.

That is training the second nature to the degree that it's automatic. But even then, the outcome is not guaranteed. Repeated, proper preparation does not guarantee the preferred outcome.

About two minutes later, Lauer quoted Carroll in a radio interview in which the coach had said, "My whole life has equipped me to deal with this moment." Referring to those disappointing moments later in the interview, Carroll said, "These don't go away. . . . they fuel me."

As the interview progressed, Lauer quoted a promise that Carroll had made to the Seahawks fan base: "We're gonna make this right."

"How do you make it right?" Lauer asked.

"By gettin' to the truth," Carroll replied. "By gettin' in there, talking about it, facin' it up, everybody's cleared their minds, and okay, this is what the truth is. And then, in time, individually, everybody feels their own way, everybody is allowed to feel exactly how they want to feel. There's nothin' wrong with that. It's when you finally gather and you're ready to take that next step, we're gonna go places that are gonna be extraordinary."

"So there's a story of redemption that you've already begun to write?" Lauer asked.

"It's well underway," Carroll answered.[4]

That, in a nutshell, is how we start our work with family businesses, by "gettin' to the truth." Is it hard? Sure, it's hard. Does it happen right away? Not usually. Just as Carroll's Seahawks couldn't have that difficult-but-necessary conversation immediately after their devastating loss, so very few family businesses feel ready to take off the cover right out of the gate. At some point, however, all of them need to uncover the truth and talk about it.

We've discovered that one of the best ways to do that is to ask the right questions. Since questions provide such a crucial piece of the discovery process, let's flesh out a good strategy for using them in the next chapter.

TWO

questions

Why do we prefer answers over questions? Do we crave certainty and the known over ambiguity and the mysterious? But if that were the case, where would science be? And what of beauty and wonder?

While it might feel "safer" to stay inside, within my known box, within my familiar worldview, within my limited perspective, staying there will never get me anywhere else. When I keep away from the mountain and avoid the ocean, I might feel safer; but I'll never watch the sun rise over a majestic peak, never mountain bike, never swim in the Pacific or take a cruise to Tahiti. Questions might not always feel safe, but they can do a wonderful job of getting us to a new and better place.

Whenever I speak to students on a topic related to career, I always ask who controls a job interview. "The interviewer," they usually respond.

"Not always," I reply. "Actually, it's the one who asks the questions."

As the conversation continues, I challenge them to become great askers of great questions.

In this chapter, I'd like to challenge you to become the same thing.

Don't Lose Sight of Wonder

In his book *A More Beautiful Question*, Warren Berger wrote, "A recent study found the average four-year-old British girl asks her poor mum 390 questions a day; the boys that age aren't far behind. . . . that age is her questioning peak."[1] He also reported, "According to Paul Harris, a Harvard child psychologist and author, research shows that a child asks about forty thousand questions between the ages of two and five."[2]

What happens *after* we peak? Why do we stop asking so many questions?

Part of it, I believe, is that we begin filling young people's minds with factoids so that they soon become gatherers of facts rather than continuing their youthful journey of questioning. Or maybe they take it to heart when we say to them as little tykes, "Daddy needs a break from your questions." And so they start asking fewer and fewer questions.

That's how we lose sight of wonder.

As we get older, we have to work harder to experience jaw-dropping awe. What used to be a natural reaction to something new and unfamiliar now seems forced. Too much programming means our imagination muscles atrophy. Oh, that we could rediscover those regular moments of wonder!

Oh, but we can. How? By asking more and better questions.

Questions and Growth

How does asking great questions help you to build a thriving family business? Let me ask a question.

Does the culture in your family business spark wonder, imagination, and *what-if* thinking? Or does your culture communicate, in one way or another, "Let me show you how to do this," and "We've always done it this way"?

Questions open things up. In today's markets, your family business has no choice but to open up. A lack of openness inevitably leads to closing in, shutting down, and atrophy. You don't want that for your business or for your family, do you?

Furthermore, it's imperative to model openness and inquiry to the next generation. Your generation and the next might survive for a time without openness and inquiry, but you won't last long, and you definitely won't thrive.

Going forward, isn't thriving what you want?

Askers or Tellers?

How effectively does your family ask questions? Are you better "askers" or "tellers"? If we want to find the truth in our journey of discovery, we have to do less telling and more asking.

Would you say you're a good listener? Try this: the next time you listen to someone, seek to understand. If you're not sure you understand, ask a clarifying question or two.

"What did you really mean when you said _____?"

"I know what I mean when I talk about ethical behavior. But what do you mean?"

"Let me make sure that I heard you correctly. Could I tell you what I heard, to make sure I understood you?"

It's okay to ask pointed questions, but make it a practice to ask open-ended questions instead of yes/no questions. Although I've gotten pretty good at asking questions over time, allow me to reveal a little "Mark dirt."

I have a natural tendency to use questions to back people into corners. I do this particularly with my wife, Lyn. When I'm trying to get her to see what she can't see, I often ask a question such as, "Did you make that call you said you were going to make?" As you might imagine, such a question does not often yield helpful results.

For Lyn, full disclosure equals honesty. When our son, Drew, was younger, he might give an honest answer to a question but fall short of full disclosure. In Drew's eyes, he was being honest, but to Lyn, not so much. When I want Lyn to see this behavior in herself, therefore, I sometimes ask questions like the one I just mentioned, which does *not* lead to openness and a thriving relationship.

Here's a basic premise: *Don't use questions to get what you want. Use questions to clarify and understand.*

Don't use questions to back people into corners. Backing people into corners closes off space. You want to use questions to open up space, to uncover the valuable ground you need to do the hard work you will later appreciate as a family and as a business.

When Drew was just four or five years old, he already had become a master at asking questions. One time as we drove with friends from the Willamette Valley to Central Oregon, Drew sat behind us in his car seat, incessantly asking questions. My friend asked, "Does he *always* ask that many questions?" I responded by turning to Drew and asking him to give it a rest—not the best move for one who now works with family businesses, encouraging them to ask great questions of each other.

Problem Solvers vs. Problem Finders

Daniel Pink, author of *Drive* and *To Sell Is Human*, stated in a blog post that we've been trained to be problem solvers. When we see a flaw, a mistake or a difficulty, we automatically tend to shift into "problem-solving" mode. We don't ask questions; we just move to find answers.[3]

If we want to move forward and thrive, however, we need to consider becoming problem *finders*. Although I'm not sure I want to know what the *National Enquirer* has to say about much of anything, its tagline is worth something: "Inquiring minds want to know." "To inquire" is another way of saying, "to ask." And "ask" implies *questions*.

Problem solvers have great value so long as they solve the right problems. But to solve those right problems, someone first has to perceive those problems—and perhaps the best way to find them is to ask a lot of questions.

Questions have a way of uncovering hidden flaws, bringing light to dark corners and making plain what has seemed invisible. For that reason, people who ask a lot of good questions—problem finders—will keep you busy for a lifetime, helping you first to perceive and then to dive into the *right* problems.

Several decades ago, the shipping industry faced what looked like an insurmountable problem. How could cargo ships get in and out of port more quickly to unload their cargo and get back on the open sea? Ports were clogging and companies were wasting tons of money. Could they get dock workers to move faster? Get bigger cranes? More cranes?

It turned out they were asking the wrong questions. They wanted to speed up the usual process; they really needed a different process. Container ships provided the answer. Why not load ships with containers full of cargo, and then just unload the containers instead of the individual pieces of cargo? Today, 90 percent of all seagoing cargo is shipped on huge container vessels. But we'd still be doing things the old, expensive, slow way if someone hadn't started asking the right questions.

Why?

If you want to get to the truth, one of the best questions to ask is, "Why?" As annoying as the question might feel when your four-year-old asks it for the thousandth time, "why" questions help us get closer to our true motivations.

Why do we want to open a fifth branch? To make more money.

Why do we want to make more money? To buy a new house.

Why do we want to buy a new house? Good question. I need to think about that.

If you really want to get to the truth, learn the value of pausing. Don't be afraid of a little silence. Don't fear the lack of an immediate, comprehensive response. "I need to think about that" must be not only an acceptable but also an encouraged response.

Veteran news gatherers regularly advise novice reporters to refrain from jumping in when a question brings nothing but silence. National Public Radio host Rachel Martin, for example, has said, "Don't be afraid of silence. Sometimes the best follow up question is to say nothing. Especially after the person has just revealed something important. More often than not, if you are quiet and give them the space to keep sharing—they will."[4]

If we never stop long enough to allow a bit of silence or to ponder a deeper answer to a "why" question, we'll continually hydroplane over our true motivators. We'll allow surface motivators to become the norm. If we don't want surface motivators to rule the day, we must give ourselves time to ponder. We need time not only to ask good questions, but time to think up even better ones.

Not So Fast!

Warren Berger cautions:

> Often the worst thing you can do with a difficult question is to try to answer it too quickly. When the mind is coming up with What If possibilities, these fresh, new ideas can take time to percolate and form. They often result from connecting existing ideas in unusual and interesting ways. Einstein was an early believer in this form of "combinatorial thinking"; today it is widely accepted as one of the primary sources of creativity. Since this type of thinking involves both connections and questions, I think of it as *connective inquiry*.[5]

I've found that the slowing down is an important practice for my clients. When we slow down, we begin to peel back the layers by asking more questions. One guy asked about his business, "Why is the 'why' so important?" The lightbulb went on for him when we started talking about future generations. His business was not just about setting money aside to be able to retire one day. The breakthrough for him came when he saw his business set into a larger context.

Good questions need to marinate. We need to take time to develop them. You've certainly heard the line that we will never get the right answer to the wrong question. So, challenge yourself to take the time to come up with good, even great, questions. You'll be glad you did.

Three Key Questions

We habitually ask business owners three questions:

1. *Is your business an asset or is it just a paycheck?* (The Value Question)

    Some construction clients ran their business out of their home. They began viewing it as an asset for the first time when we began talking about a helpful separation between business and personal concerns. We discussed moving the office out of their home. They bought a building and remodeled it. Only then did they begin to see the company as an asset rather than as a paycheck.

2. *Do you produce or provide something that should outlive you?* (The Generation Question)

    "I've always thought of the business as my retirement," a client told me. But when you challenge that way of thinking, it can prompt someone to start thinking beyond just himself. What is it to think generationally?

    Do any of us really "own" anything? Or are we caretakers for a period of time, then we hand off the enterprise? Or maybe we need to say, "This is just for a season. Is there a way for the business to die well?"

3. *Can you envision greater things in the next generation?* (The Legacy Question)

As we worked through a change of roles in one family business, a second-generation dad told his children, "In five years, I probably won't be around here as much. Things will probably look a lot different than if I had stuck around. But that's okay with me." In speaking in this way, he made a hugely liberating statement about them taking the business where they thought it should go.

The elder generation can build confidence into the younger generation that they really can do something special and make it work. What could happen if the elders in your business seriously considered this approach? You could say, "Let's dream a little. What could the business look like? Have you guys begun to think what that might look like?"

Good Things Happen

Good things happen when you make questioning a part of your culture. Good questions open up space that causes us to continue to think rather than to shut down.

While a statement can bring an ending, we never want to stop the conversation. If we use questions to keep the conversation going, we'll get somewhere good.

THREE

▼

conflict

I still remember the referral phone call that connected me with one of my clients. The referring party described a conflict-laden situation and then asked if I might be interested in working with the men involved. In knee-jerk style, I said yes.

On my way to our first meeting, however, I began to wonder what I'd gotten myself into. Conflict in this business had grown so nasty that the two family-member owners had completely stopped speaking to one another. It didn't help that their small office featured an open design, which meant that other employees could both see and hear virtually everything that was going on. I went to the meeting anyway and by its end, we decided to move forward.

At our second meeting, we had arranged to execute the formal agreement. As I sat there, ready to sign paperwork, I remember thinking, "I'm not sure I want to do this." At that very moment, the warring family members had begun hammering at each other, scrapping tooth and nail. Accusations, innuendos, uncontrolled emotions—it all spilled out on the table, joining the unsigned paperwork.

I soon discovered that this volatile situation had begun to unravel about six months earlier when Dad had died. Before his death, Dad had always stepped in to break the tie any time a decision had to be made involving the two squabbling family members. And now Dad was gone.

As you might imagine, decision-making in this family business had become explosive, and some of the decisions that got made anyway created even more conflict.

Whenever conflict in a family business erupts, I've noticed that the warring parties typically start to make all kinds of unwarranted assumptions. And what's true about assumptions in general only gets magnified regarding assumptions made during a conflict; they're usually dead wrong. If you want a recipe for disaster, try to operate in a culture dominated by false assumptions.

That's the toxic culture I walked into when I began working with this client.

In our early conversations, we had to employ the "feather method" (although we used a mini football instead). Maybe you've heard of this approach. Whoever holds the feather has the floor; they get to speak until they feel understood. Once they believe they've been thoroughly heard and understood, they can pass the feather (or the football) to the other person. Using this tactic helped us to slow things down, cools things off, open some ears, and begin some needed conversation. As understanding began to take place, the participants slowly began to jettison their belief that talking to one another was futile. Eventually they came to believe that conversation could continue and even prove mutually beneficial.

In time, the two sparring family members realized that they

actually *did* have some common ground. They admitted that they missed being "just family," as they remembered special holiday times spent together, enjoying one another's company.

Together we began to develop what we call a Cultural Covenant (I deal more extensively with Cultural Covenants in chapter 16). They realized that if they couldn't vote in unison, especially when they had to make important decisions, that meant they needed more conversation. This became one of the "commandments" in their Cultural Covenant, a short list of agreed-upon nonnegotiables. Once a Cultural Covenant goes public, anyone in the organization can refer back to the covenant whenever conflict rears its head.

This little story confirms for me what Jeremy Statton, an orthopedic surgeon by day and a blogger by night, once wrote: "Conflict is the catalyst for action resulting in change."[1] When I helped these family members face their conflict, they took positive action that changed the course of the future in their individual, family, and business lives.

One day, after we had walked a good distance into the process, I asked them, "What if you end up here again?" One of the two had an interesting response. "We'll *never* end up here again," he declared. "We have too much at stake."

Two Sources of Conflict

I believe that two major sources fuel most of our conflicts: misunderstanding and selfishness. We have to deal with each in differing ways. Let's briefly look at the second source first.

Selfishness leads to conflict because we don't get what we want, and that makes us angry. How do you solve conflict generated by selfishness? It's simple but very hard. You have to confess, "I didn't get my own way, so I got mad and took it out on you," or "I got angry and I grabbed my ball and went home." No one likes making such an admission, but it's really the only way to cut the ground out from under selfishness.

Andy Stanley gave a series of talks called "Future Family" in which he asked what causes fights and quarrels among us. "Do you know why you hurt the people closest to you the most?" he asked, then answered, "Because they're close to *you*." Stanley suggested pointing to the person with whom you're having the conflict and saying, "You know what part of the problem is right now? I'm not getting what I want," and then pointing to yourself. Stanley says that when we own our part of the issue, we lose leverage. And then we should ask the other person, "Who is suffering because I'm not getting my own way?"[2]

We need to ask, "What is *my* role in this problem?" Even if my part is only 1 percent of the problem, how can I take 100 percent responsibility for my 1 percent? More than once I've seen clients try to blame a business blowup completely on another sibling or person in the company, while I know the person is responsible for *at least* 1 percent of the problem. We need to look in the mirror instead of a microscope.

The basic way to deal with the second source of conflict, *misunderstanding*, is to clarify the situation. If I didn't understand what you said, what should I do? I need to ask questions.

Misunderstanding often leads to false assumptions, incorrect assumptions can lead to bad conclusions, and bad conclusions frequently express themselves in "always" and "never" statements: "You always . . ." or "You never . . ." When we start talking like that to one another, conflict always follows.

In my experience with family businesses, I can say categorically that most conflict that results from misunderstanding is unnecessary. When we sit down to think about it, we see that much of the conflict we experience comes from simple misunderstanding:

"I thought you said, 'Go to hell!'"

"No, I said, 'Ring the bell!'"

My dad said to me many times, "Mark, you're not hard of hearing. You're just hard of listening."

Listen! Listen! Listen! And when you think you've listened really well, ask the speaker if she feels heard. If not, listen some more. If she does feel heard, I'll bet you've just avoided some unnecessary conflict.

Signs of Conflict

What signs indicate that conflict may exist in your business? I can think of several:

- *Giving the silent treatment.*
  You're as cold as ice. You say nothing, even if addressed. Doctors might as well have sewn your lips shut.

- *Stifling healthy disagreement or refusing to discuss clear problem areas.*
  Some individuals avoid conflict by bleaching red flags white. They see trouble ahead (red flags flapping in the wind), but they keep quiet about it (they take the red flags down and bleach them white). While the outcome of doing this kind of "laundry" is self-evident, what does such conflict avoidance end up costing in the end? Far more than the few coins we might dispense in visiting the laundromat!

- *Making snide comments.*
  "Any more bright ideas, sunshine? Your last one worked out *grrrreat.*"

- *Avoiding the person.*
  You see him coming down the hall toward you, and instead of continuing your planned march to the lunch room, suddenly you feel an irresistible urge to duck into the restroom.

- *Making decisions unilaterally.*
  Why should you speak with *her*? She'll only go negative on you, anyway. Better just to make the decision yourself.

- *Making no decisions at all.*
  Maybe if we just avoid making the decision, the problem will go away on its own.

- *Failing to dream about the future.*
  Conflicting visions of the future can spark conflict. Sometimes to avoid that conflict, one party spends no time developing her own vision for the future, since it can feel easier to avoid such thinking (or that type of conversation) in order to keep the peace. But you know what often happens, don't you? By trying to avoid the conflict, you end up causing far more damage down the road.

Do you recognize any of these signs of conflict in your own business? If so, understand that unresolved conflict doesn't have to create a barrier to relationship. Conflict in style doesn't have to lead to conflict in relationship. And even when conflicts erupt, I have to tell you that I'm okay with sparks flying—so long as they ignite a "controlled burn" and not a wildfire.

Too Valuable to Waste

"A crisis is a terrible thing to waste," insisted Dick Clark, CEO at Merck.[3] It really is. And a crisis sparked by conflict is just as terrible to waste.

Think about your own team for a moment. How does it handle conflict, whether individually or collectively? Do some team members avoid conflict, while others appear to cause it?

In a recent meeting with a client, it became clear to me that the physical temperature of the office had become a sharp point of contention. Some wanted the windows perpetually open, while others brought out the sweaters and switched on the space heaters as soon as someone even mentioned turning on the air conditioning or opening a window.

Just as we have personal preferences on where to set the thermostat, so we all have a personal preference when it comes to setting the conflict thermostat. Some set it on zero: they tolerate no conflict at all. The moment conflict raises its head, these individuals are outta there. Others seem to thrive on conflict—the hotter, the better.

Everyone involved, including those at both extremes and those in between, needs to realize that wherever they set this conflict thermostat tends to communicate to others something very different from what they intend. If you usually find yourself in someone else's face during a confrontation, for example (or even when discussing an important matter), realize that you're probably communicating intense hostility. The other party may believe you're saying to them, "You'd better be afraid. Be *very* afraid!" On the other hand, if you immediately flee during a conflict, you can unintentionally communicate personal disinterest, even regarding critical matters. Lack of engagement can inhibit good communication just as much as in-your-face confrontation.

I've come to believe that conflict, properly handled, can actually strengthen your business and bring it to the next level. Conflict can bring something incredibly valuable to the table *if* you learn how to use it well.

Or even better, if you learn to mine it effectively.

Mine That Ore!

Do you think it's reasonable to say, "There's valuable ore in that conflict somewhere, and we'll find it if we keep digging"? Do you view conflict in this way—as something valuable to be mined—or do you see it as something to avoid at all costs?

I grew up in a family where Mom and Dad never tried to hide their fights. Unfortunately, I also never saw them resolve their conflicts. I think that's why I went into marriage with a determination never to fight.

The good Lord must know what's best, because I married a feisty (in a very good way!) woman, and Lyn refused to allow me *not* to fight. My determination to avoid conflict might have made it through our honeymoon, but not much further. And so I learned to fight.

And fight we can.

That's not my natural bent. I've always desired to quickly eliminate conflict, not mine it. Maybe it's because I've heard the apostle Paul whispering to me, "Don't let the sun go down on your anger." Whatever the case, my habit has gotten me into trouble more than once. Over the years, however, I've learned that before we can mine the conflict and so defuse it, sometimes we need to let things cool down a bit. We have to first inject some cooling air into an overheated atmosphere. Lately I've even come to realize that, at least in my lifetime, some conflict can't (or won't) be resolved. This is new ground for me, and I have to learn to live with it.

It helps me to know that even those kinds of conflicts can be mined for valuable ore.

So if we consent that conflict *will* happen and that it's not all bad, can we become good miners of conflict? Can we take the right pickaxes, the right canaries, and the right headlamps and helmets into the mine with us? I believe we can.

William Bridges, in his book *The Way of Transition*, described his marriage to Mondi, who died of breast cancer. "Mondi's and my marriage was a rich and rewarding one," he wrote. "But the intimacy of that last year grew out of soil that was rich and deep not only from happy years together but also from the decay of our countless fallen hopes."[4] Such a perspective mines a terrible conflict. And persistent miners find valuable ore, sometimes even the mother lode.

As good as that is, I think it's possible to go even one step further. How would you respond if I asked if it might be possible to profitably mine *for* conflict?

"What an odd question," you might think.

But maybe not.

Suppose that I had stuck to my guns early in marriage and had refused to fight with my wife. What would have happened? More importantly, what *wouldn't* have happened? If disagreement never erupts in a marriage or a family or a business, what gets missed? What won't get discovered if no sparks fly?

My wife recently had separate conversations with each of our adult children. Neither of them have married yet, but both independently expressed to Lyn a desire to find a marriage partner who would "engage" the way they've seen Lyn and me engage. By "engage," I mean "fight," and believe me, they've seen us engage. The kids even served as our referees at times. Yet they didn't see our engagements as negative. They not only saw them but they want what we have.

I doubt we have ever received a greater compliment. I hope that because we've "engaged" in front of our children, we've given them a good example of mining—mining conflict as well as mining *for* conflict. For that kind of mining to produce good ore, however, I've also learned that we need to understand and put into practice two critically important principles.

Principle #1: Forgiveness, Key to the Future

While it may seem difficult to think about forgiveness in the midst of intense conflict, eventually we need to put forgiveness on the table. Actress Janine Turner once told an interviewer that she had read through the Bible the previous year and could summarize her reading in two ways: "Don't judge," and "I'm forgiven to the degree I forgive."[5]

What if we took both of Turner's insights to the table of conflict? What would happen if we refrained from judging? And what would happen if we took the lead in extending forgiveness? Forgiveness is a powerful force whether we withhold it or extend it, but it's infinitely more potent when we offer it to those who have hurt us.

In the same interview, Turner spoke of some women who had suffered deep wounds from brutal oppressors. She said the women had learned to become "stewards of their wounds."[6] What a fascinating phrase!

When I'm hurt or wounded in some conflict, do I work to become a caretaker of those wounds? Am I willing to let those wounds do some deep and profound work in *me*? Am I willing to let those wounds "heal" others?

How can we become stewards of our wounds rather than their prisoners? One way to change our perspective about conflict is to realize that conflict happens and people often get hurt by it, but we can choose to extend forgiveness and so become stewards of our wounds rather than their prisoners.

As apartheid began to crumble in South Africa, Desmond Tutu helped oversee the South African Truth and Reconciliation Commission, a group tasked with calling out the wrongs committed over decades and making restitution wherever possible. If true confession had taken place, the commission could have offered a form of amnesty. But regardless, the members of the commission had each committed themselves to move forward in forgiveness and reconciliation. While many Africans had suffered unspeakable atrocities, the power of forgiveness won the day in uncounted miraculous ways.

Out of these profound experiences, Archbishop Tutu wrote a landmark book with a title both provocative and prophetic: *No Future Without Forgiveness*. In it he wrote,

> A recent issue of the journal *Spirituality and Health* had on its front cover a picture of three US ex-servicemen standing in front of the Vietnam Memorial in Washington, D.C. One asks, "Have you forgiven those who held you prisoner of war?" "I will never forgive them," replies the other. His mate says: "Then it seems they still have you in prison, don't they?"[7]

Forgiveness opens these prison doors.

I stood on holy ground one morning as I listened to two former business partners explain their own versions of what had broken their business. One partner had left to pursue another venture, which had caused the other partner some serious problems.

While the men had made attempts to maintain their relationship after the business breakup, each former partner had experienced his own stages of grief. Both men originally envisioned remaining partners "forever," ultimately riding off into the sunset together. But that vision cracked, broke, and crumbled into dust.

As they communicated less and less with each other over time, one partner came to think that his former partner had become "stuck" somewhere, perhaps in anger. The two men eventually asked me to serve as a mediator.

As we met to see whether the pair could achieve some kind of reconciliation, these former partners listened intently as I read a letter that the "leaver" had written in response to a letter penned by the one who had remained. With tears in my eyes, I watched the partner who had stayed apologize for things he had said in that first letter—some of his own personal "stuff," no doubt a reflection of his deep grief over the loss of the partnership.

As I watched and then reflected on this "holy ground" moment, I thought, "This is the way life is supposed to work. When conflict occurs, as it inevitably will, let confession, forgiveness, and healing do their work!"

Sometime later, I had the privilege of meeting with all of the former and current partners along with their spouses. So often partners take home only *their* version of what has transpired, and so much gets lost in translation. The poorly translated messages almost inevitably result in either a "stand by your man" posturing by the spouse, or resentment, or both. And these warped translations typically strain relationships, widening already existing gaps.

As I met with these partners and their spouses, I first offered some thoughts on forgiveness. Near the end of the meeting, one spouse restated a parable Jesus had told thousands of years before. He had described a group of workers, hired at various times throughout the day, who at the end all got paid the same amount.[8] "At times," she said, "life just doesn't seem fair"—and yet, the inequalities don't have to cripple relationships.

After she spoke, the members of the group collectively acknowledged the incredible relationships that still existed among them, and they all agreed that no money or business deal was going to break them. They spoke excitedly of the culture that existed in the office and outside of the office, in relationships both personal and professional.

More holy ground!

When I first walked into that partner/spouse meeting, I frankly saw no way forward. But when there seemed no way, a way emerged. A new light bulb went on. And forgiveness led the way.

While this incident may seem like a rarity in business, I can assure you that it happened. And in my view, its kind needs to multiply.

Principle #2: Hope Keeps Us Alive

Whenever conflict emerges, don't forget to keep hope alive—because when hope dies, a host of other things die along with it. If you keep hope alive, you *will* find a way.

Embers of hope have to be kept alive even through the darkest of times. But maybe, just maybe, psychiatrist Gerald May is right. He wrote in *The Dark Night of the Soul* that this "darkness" may not be bad, but rather just a place where "all things are obscured."[9] If we continue to remain hopeful, a compelling vision of the way forward may one day emerge. And then the light can shine out of the darkness.

For that vision to emerge, however, first we may have to endure some personal suffering. Nobody learns perseverance without learning from the teacher we call suffering! In a paradoxical way, hope can actually grow *stronger* in these dark times. And ultimately, hope does not disappoint.

I've been in a lot of heated conversations with clients, to the point where people threatened to walk out the door. That threat can often lead to an ultimatum: "If you walk out the door, you're done." Happily, I've also seen people not walk out the door, thus restoring a new sense of hope, simply by persevering. A breakthrough appears, taking them to a new place they've never been, full of hope and possibility.

Elephants in the Room

Before I wrap up this discussion about conflict in family businesses, I need to mention one last issue. We've all experienced what we call "elephants in the room." Everyone knows when some big point of conflict has lumbered into the room, shaken its great bulk, and sat down in the middle of the floor—but no one dares to say anything about it.

Elephants are real. They are big. And if they are in the room, they stink.

Did you know that the term *white elephant* comes from a legend about the King of Siam (now Thailand)? It's said that he gave such animals to his enemies in order to ruin the recipients through the exorbitant cost of maintaining the gift. Both perceived and real conflicts act like these elephants.

When someone is living in a room we own (and they're not family), usually they are tenants; they pay rent to us, the owners. Elephants are the only tenants I know that not only don't pay us rent, but they *charge* us rent. Don't let them! Call them for what they are: stinkin' squatters!

We need to keep an eye out for these elephants. Ask yourself, "How many elephants are in the room? Are any of them hiding out? How long have they been around?" Once you recognize their presence, try to make appropriate fun of them:

"Look at that big white thing with the pink bow tie! How'd *she* get in here?"

Whenever you think you detect the presence of an elephant, ask the others in the room, "Can we admit that an elephant is in this room? Is now a good time to talk about the elephant in the room?" Once you've addressed the elephant, evict her. And don't kid yourself—these animals show up more often than we realize. Most importantly, don't let yourself become an elephant breeder!

Gifts in Odd Packages

One family business client made an incredible statement about the kind of "bad stuff" that often comes with conflict. "We get to the point where we view these things as gifts," she said.

That's how I want to view *my* conflicts! When we start to see conflict as something we can use to move the family business forward—and not as something to avoid, or ignore, or muzzle—then we can begin to make progress. Not all gifts come in pretty packages! It's what's inside that counts. And when we recognize and use conflict for the gift that it is, we lavish on ourselves one of the biggest-ticket presents available.

- part two -

IDENTIFY

CLARIFY AND PRIORITIZE
THE ISSUES TO ADDRESS

FOUR

▼

family issues

"This family business thing would be easy if it weren't for the people."

Have you ever heard someone say something like that? And then there are the issues surrounding the business itself (we'll get to that in a bit).

Here's the teeter totter: How do you balance family and business? And how should we define "family"? Should we include in-laws? How about "outlaws"?

In my experience, *all* small businesses are really *family* businesses. I'm a part of one and have been for twenty years. Lyn and I moved back to my college town to be a part of the business when my partner, Dan, and his wife decided, "We want to share our business and our revenue with the Wickmans." Over these last two decades, Dan has said many times, "You're family." And it's true. While we are not blood, we've come to be "family."

Family. Business. Two words. Almost always, one word outweighs the other. Sometimes family comes first, and sometimes business wins out. Sometimes with two partners, the one you'd think would emphasize family instead tips to the business end, and sometimes the one you'd expect to gravitate toward business ends up prioritizing family.

Which hat do you wear most often? I can change hats midsentence. I jokingly asked a client who creates custom clothing to make me two hats, one that says "Family" and one that says "Business." That's the teeter totter. And it can get tough to stay on it.

Family First?

Always remember: while the story of your family business may have an ending, the story of your family won't.

A couple of years ago, we traveled abroad and spent time with a couple in France. They had several businesses and a large family. We ended up in a long conversation about sibling conflict, transition, laws, advisors, and related issues. They recounted their concern about the way a son-in-law had "set his sights" on the family business, how he seemed to want to take over. The mom said she had seen another situation in which a son-in-law "took the place" of the eldest son, which took a huge toll on that eldest son.

In your family business, should anything like that ever happen? Should an in-law ever be allowed to take the place of a blood family member? Here's my advice: *Tread lightly here.* Never say never, but if you want the best for your kids (and most parents do), and if you feel a bit disappointed in your eldest son, *don't* arbitrarily or hastily replace him with a son-in-law. If you do, you run a great risk of damaging your relationship with your son—and that's a risk you can never completely quantify ahead of time.

You could "ruin" your son without intending to do so. And if you do this, realize that you will violate the order of the words *family business*.

Don't do that! You cannot pay *that* price for the business.

Having said all of that, you *can* carefully employ a son-in-law. You can even pass the leadership baton to a son-in-law or a daughter-in-law. We have a client who did just that. I interviewed Mom and Dad and asked who should carry the baton. I interviewed their three biological kids along with the son-in-law. *All* of them said that the son-in-law was the right "heir apparent" to run the business for the next leg of the race. That should make it easy, right?

Not so fast. It became clear that Mom and Dad felt afraid to tell the kids. Why? They didn't want to communicate that their biological children weren't up to the task. They thought that such a message would leave a damaging, lasting mark on their kids.

At the same time, the adult children felt afraid to tell Mom and Dad that the son-in-law was "the guy." Why? They didn't want to suggest to their parents that they didn't value the business or want to run it. They didn't want to let Mom and Dad down.

How, then, does such a ticklish problem get resolved? I can tell you how this one was resolved.

As I drove to meet with the team—Mom, Dad, the kids, and the son-in-law—I pondered our predicament. I knew Dad couldn't bring the message to the team. I knew the son-in-law couldn't either. So, after talking to the son-in-law, I called the eldest son, asking if he'd bring the message. He agreed to do so.

When the eldest son declared in front of the whole team that the younger generation believed the son-in-law should receive the baton, you could instantly observe the change in Dad. Immediate physical relief!

A word to the wise: if you are considering moving down this track, let me urge you to *start the conversation early*. In fact, *real* early!

The Enemy Is . . . Us?

Let's return to France for a moment. Mom and Dad felt sad because they didn't see their kids emerging with the will or the means to continue the family business. In 2008, they thought they had sold the company. The intended sale even made it into the press and an event was scheduled to celebrate the new ownership; but with everything signed, the buyer died in a tragic accident. The parents took this tragedy as a sign.

As all of this was happening, they also made an offer on some property in a different part of France. The property owner, a man in his eighties, got angry (even though he'd spent considerable time trying to sell and now appeared about to get what he wanted), grew ill, and ended up dying in the hospital.

Can you guess Mom and Dad's conclusion? *Don't buy or sell with our family.*

Since then, they've tried three separate family meetings led by three different mediators: a consultant "selling" some financial products, an attorney, and a notary. They've had little success with any of the three. Finally, they told me, "We need a Mark." But that hasn't gone anywhere either.

Herein lies one of the most common, most difficult dilemmas that family businesses face: they aren't aware of the trouble they're heading into until they're already in it.

Have you ever heard of someone calling for a tow truck before he landed in the ditch? I haven't either. My experience with family businesses tells me that they work in a similar way. They don't call for outside help until they find themselves in the ditch. I wish it were different, but it hardly ever is.

Before we go any further, allow me to place some of the blame for this ditch landing squarely on the shoulders of people like me. I'm now in the "elder" category, and part of our problem was stated well many years ago by the wise cartoon character Pogo:
We've met the enemy, and he is us.
So what can we do about that?

The Most Difficult Question

Although we already discussed the general issue of questions in chapter 2, let me name the question that, in my experience, is by far the most difficult for family businesses to answer. The question is always directed at the one "at the helm," whether that's the founder or the company elder. The most difficult question to answer with any kind of specificity is this:
"What do you want to do?"
I've been involved in situations where that question has been asked for decades without once getting an answer. Why is that question so hard for many elders? While I can imagine many possible reasons, let me mention just two.

1. Letting go

A family business can feel an awful lot like a child, particularly for the founder but also for a loyal follower. You've raised it. You've changed its diapers. You've nursed it back to health. It's also something like a marriage: *In sickness and in health, in good times and bad, till death do us part.* Letting go is hard, if not impossible, for most elders.

All family businesses have to answer The Generational Question and The Legacy Question (see chapter 2) and similar ones, but to get a definitive answer to any of them, the elder must let go. Too many elders "die with their boots on," to the detriment of the business, the family, and even themselves.

Fear is a great motivator for most of us. Fear can hold us captive. For many elders, the fear of letting go keeps them from answering the question, "What do you want to do?"

Susan Sokol Blosser, a pioneer in the Oregon wine industry, recently wrote a great book titled *Letting Go*. She chronicled her challenges as a founder through the wilderness of letting go. What a difficult journey! She described a major turning point when, on a trip, she broke her ankle. Her daughter had to step in and give a business presentation, and after they returned home, Susan had to sit and watch "the kids" run the business. She called it one of the best things that ever could have happened to accelerate the healthy transition process.[1]

2. Identity

Elders, particularly boomers and those of earlier generations, have put virtually all of their blood, sweat, and tears into their businesses. If the business succeeds, the elder often sits on multiple boards, is considered a pillar in his community, gets asked to speak as an expert on myriad topics, and on it goes. Travel often includes a convention or visiting a key client or additional travel with other business owners. Does the elder have a life apart from business?

Speaking of travel, if she does travel, who goes with her? Very often, her traveling companions are family members who work with her in the business. And so in some out-of-the-way nook in some far-flung corner of the globe, a frightening thought eventually hits the elder: "Who am I if I no longer own this business?" Later we'll discuss ways to keep the retired elder engaged, but for now, think for a moment about the consequences of a disengaged elder who still wants to call the shots.

I doubt those thoughts fill you with peace and joy.

The elder/founder also faces another dilemma. He or she probably has an entrepreneurial spirit. And what is true of the entrepreneur? To succeed, the entrepreneur must not listen to naysayers. Innovative businesses that survive and thrive usually had an entrepreneurial founder who put his head down and put blinders on. So then, when the time comes to venture into this new territory of transitioning out, he can often employ the same skills he used to make the business successful in the first place: head down, blinders on, not listening.

You get the picture.

But all founders need to hear an important news flash: *What it took to get you where you are today is not what it will take to get you where you want to go.* In fact, those same skills will almost certainly get in the way of successful succession.

Denise Kenyon-Rouvinez and John Ward authored an insightful book titled *Family Business Key Issues*. In it, they addressed the founder's identity: "Founders have been neither followers nor successors. Most entrepreneurs are very control-oriented. For a founder to step down before the issue is forced biologically is often a threat to his or her existence. The business may be the founder's identity, passion, and primary means of fulfillment."[2]

If you try to address a family business succession without dealing with the founder's/elder's identity, you are likely in for a rough ride indeed.

Other Family Members

So far I've focused on the founder/elder, but let's give her a break. We also have other family members to consider. Let's start with those married to the elders.

1. Spouses

Some family businesses employ spouses, some do not, and there may be no rhyme or reason when it comes to "giving" spouses a job in a family business. We regularly say there is a difference between giving someone a voice and giving them a vote. Stock ownership aside, some voices try to become voters. They want to make decisions. That is natural.

In the introduction, I mentioned that I helped to start a church. We had at least four senior pastors in a span of less than a decade. Somehow, it fell to me to try to lead the mediation of some of those challenging conversations, sometimes involving spouses. I discovered, after ending up in my own "ditch" several times, that occasionally the organization needs to involve non-working spouses in conversations on a need-to-know basis. If it fails to do this, the leadership group becomes the villain, whether or not it merits the characterization. After a difficult meeting, the "worker" goes home and the spouse asks, "How'd it go?" And then the unloading begins. It's perfectly natural for the spouse to develop a "stand-by-your-man" (or your woman) attitude.

But there's always more to the story.

With clients, we now try to involve spouses early on in crucial conversations. The non-working spouse, in particular, needs access to the same crucial information (usually non-financial) so that when the couple processes that information, they can do so with a degree of objectivity not possible if the sole perspective comes from the working spouse. Because opposites so often attract, it can help to have that unique perspective and differing way of processing information as part of a conversation involving key issues related to family and business.

2. Kids

While we will discuss governance issues later in this book (questions such as, "Must the kids work elsewhere before joining the family business?"), it's important to raise the issue of kids here if we're to have healthy conversations regarding the future of the family business.

Children in family businesses are subject to a sort of double-edged sword. A family business might foster a sense of excitement or, on the other hand, it may seem like too big a cross to bear; some children dislike the pressure of having to carry on what Mom and Dad have built.

Entitlement is another risk. It can be part of what never gets spoken, whether within the family or within the non-family part of the business. I'll say this: if you want to put multiple people and situations at great risk, even the business and the family itself, then don't talk about it.

Kids in a family business raise a host of topics that *must* be addressed: hiring practices, at what age various jobs/roles can be taken on, wages, bonuses, stock ownership, authority, and accountability to company policy, to name a few. Once addressed, the results must be communicated not only to family, but to the whole company. Failure to thoroughly communicate with all concerned parties can put the whole enterprise at risk, but that's one risk that can be mitigated by a healthy business culture.

A couple of years ago, after having several meetings with a father, we decided to set up a lunch with his two kids who worked in the business. Dad said he would let his kids decide if they wanted to hire me to help facilitate their crucial conversations relating to transition issues. We had the lunch. My read was that the kids wanted to move forward with my help. Shortly thereafter, however, I heard from Dad that they were going to hold off because the business faced some tough staffing and financial decisions. Not long after, Dad told me they were not going to hire me. He also informed me that his daughter had left the business. Dad interpreted her decision to leave as her desire to pursue her own venture.

But I wonder...

I've seen elders give a "gift" to their kids—in this case, the authority to make a decision whether to hire a facilitator—only to take back the gift. Don't do that to your kids! And kids, if you observe that kind of behavior in your elders, call them on it. Letting it slide will not lead to a healthy culture.

Common Family Issues

In such a small book I can't possibly mention all the significant family issues inherent in family businesses, but let me summarize a few of the most common ones. You may well recognize your own situation in one of the following brief scenarios.

- *The bad assumption.* A farmer wants to retire and assumes (that awful word again!) the eldest of his three sons will move back home to take over the farm. The son, however, wants to live in another state and become a basketball coach. Where does the son get the courage to talk to Dad? Or because the son heard Dad say, "I moved back to help out *my* mom and dad on the farm, and I just figured you'd do the same," does he say nothing and resent the farm (and Dad) for the rest of his life?

- *The boomerang.* Mom comes in one day to the business and announces, "I'm done, girls! Here are the keys to the company store. It's yours!" But the next day she's back in the store, looking over her daughter's shoulder, saying, "I'm not sure I'd do it that way." The daughters never take risks for fear that "Mom wouldn't do it that way." And what is the price tag on not taking appropriate, even necessary risks?

- *The prodigal returns.* One of the sons left some time ago, and now he says, "I want to come back. I promise, I'm here to stay." But is he? How can the other siblings trust him? How can they talk about this, get their cards on the table, and let go of the resentment they feel toward him and toward Mom and Dad for welcoming him back with open arms? (On this issue I highly recommend Henri Nouwen's book, *The Return of the Prodigal Son.*)

- *Our nuclear family vs. our business family.* More than thirty years ago, a college classmate of mine started a business that today employs more than eighty people. Those people are "family." He and his wife also have three kids, all of whom have some sort of involvement in the business. He wonders, "Do they have the energy, ability, and desire to lead this?" He also wonders how to process another thought: "I'm not sure if I *want* this for my kids."

- *Good cop/bad cop.* How can Dad and Mom become aware of the strong tendency parents have to fall into the "good cop/bad cop" routine with their kids? I've discovered that an unforeseen outcome of this routine is almost inevitably a "cop fight."

The big question to ask is how your family business can become a source of *unity* for your family. How can your family business actually become part of the family legacy, the positive heritage you want to pass on and that your kids want to gratefully carry on? One thing is for sure: it won't happen by accident.

A Braver Man in All of Us

A couple of years ago my wife and I started watching a show on Netflix called *Parenthood*. Producer Ron Howard and his cohorts use the show to brilliantly address all kinds of contemporary family issues.

They set the show in the Bay Area, where the Braverman family is exposed in all of their guts and glory (sometimes that should read "gory"). The eldest son is a something of a rock, but his wife battles cancer and they have a son with Asperger's. The family faces multiple challenging relationships, divorces, adoptions, job losses, identity crises, and on and on it goes. The show addresses a host of thorny issues, among them social justice, abortion, politics, and an empty nest that gets repopulated with adult children. What we all face, right? But they put it all out there, on the screen, in living color.

Do you and I put our "stuff" out there for the world to see? It's so easy to think that we're the only ones challenged with thorny issues in this family business. But that's the power of the secret! One of the many cool things about *Parenthood* is that the cast and crew help break the power of the secret. They put their "stuff" out there—and their stuff is my stuff and your stuff.

One of the Braverman daughters, Sarah, is a single mom. Her ex-husband battled the demons of drugs and alcohol as a struggling musician, staying constantly on the road and, for the most part, out of his kids' lives. Mom does her best but often seems to be her own worst enemy (who among us can't play *that* character?). She bounces from relationship to relationship and from job to job, always torpedoing anything good that comes her way, as though she's convinced she doesn't deserve anything good.

Eventually Sarah Braverman discovers she is a pretty decent photographer. She "steals" a job from a former employer/lover and then questions whether she's up to the task. Her current love interest tells her, "You're not in over your head. You're just out of your comfort zone."[3]

Those two lines stopped me in my tracks. How often have we played the mental tape that we're in over our head, prompting us to let go of a dream or an opportunity? But what if, as that tape plays, another tape started playing, saying something very different: "You're not in over your head. You're just out of your comfort zone"?

What risks have I chosen not to take, simply because I believed I was in over my head?

Or maybe it's just that I *like* my comfort zone. Maybe I don't like anyone or anything messing with my comfort zone. And so, I take no risks . . . and therefore, I miss the reward.

Frankly, I've been challenged lately on risk. I know I need to take more. When my comfort zone calls my name, I need to remember those great lines from *Parenthood*: "You're not in over your head. You're just out of your comfort zone."

Were I to follow this advice, I too might become a Braver Man. How about you? How about your family? Your business? What risks have you failed to take, or even to consider, because you knew they'd take you out of your comfort zone? Do any of them relate to identifying the key issues you know you need to address but have so far avoided because of the pain you knew they'd cause?

Identifying the crucial issues in your family business doesn't create those issues—it merely brings them into the light, where you can finally deal with them effectively. So take the risk. Identify them, clarify them, and prioritize them. Don't let a little fear, or even a little pain, keep you from taking that necessary risk.

You're not in over your head. You're just out of your comfort zone.

FIVE

generations

> A generation is a group of people
> who are programmed at the same time in history.
>
> *Author Unknown*

About a year ago, my daughter, Lindsay, now in her midtwenties, started dating a new guy. Lyn and I had the privilege of spending some time with the couple. Since I'm glad to say that Lindsay still respects my opinion, she asked me, "What do you think of him?"

Wanting to be honest and at the same time respect my daughter's wisdom and good judgment, I thought a bit before I replied.

"Lindsay," I said, "there are three categories of things I observe. First, there are generational differences." (They had rented bikes, which Lindsay had paid for; that probably wouldn't have happened when Lyn and I were dating. The four of us later went out to eat, and even though Lindsay and her date knew that Lyn and I were treating, in my day I would have offered to help pay, at least.)

"Second, there are personality or personal preferences." (He didn't appear to like biking as much as Lindsay or I did.)

"Third, there are character issues. You know him better than I do and so are way more qualified to pass any kind of judgment, if you do at all, on his character."

Many times I think I tend to twist personal preference and generational issues into character issues. Be careful with this one! When businesses get to the transition stage, we all have to deal with enough hot water without pouring the contents of a boiling cauldron into the mix.

As we consider the very real differences between generations, is it any wonder that family businesses face challenges when trying to communicate, plan, and transition intergenerationally? Through the years, many observers have noted a number of traits that tend to characterize family businesses and the generations represented in them. Let's take a look.

The Founder Generation

The founder generation seems like a good place to start. Most likely, the founder had (or has) an entrepreneurial spirit. Maybe more than one family member possesses that spirit, which lives on in either a dream or a sense of calling or maybe both.

We've already seen how some elders, many of whom are founders, tend to behave (see chapter 4). We know that the "tunnel vision" of most founders produces both good and bad results, reminding us that strength unbridled inevitably becomes weakness. A strong, singular focus comes with its own set of blind spots! Even a bit of self-awareness can aid greatly as a founder contemplates the future and tries to work constructively with the subsequent generation to establish a good foundation for future success.

Eventually, every founder becomes an elder—and I've observed a number of common "elder errors":

- *Elders often miss requests, or don't meet them, for facilitated conversation.*

Elders often have a hard time believing that "the truth" won't come out unless a skilled and impartial mediator is present to help guide the discussion.

- *Elders have a great wariness about getting help.*

They often will wonder out loud, "For crying out loud, how tough can talking be? Nobody needs to help me 'talk'!"

- *Elders use only one set of eyes—theirs—to look at things.*

When elders don't rely on other sets of eyes and tap the wisdom available to them through a different perspective, they lose "depth perception." The elder can't see things in 3-D. The situation remains in a flat-world state, and so he or she misses the richness available to anyone with 3-D vision.

- *Elders don't talk.*

This is especially true of the Depression-era generation. Talking didn't help them out of their poverty—work did. And you work best with your mouth closed.

- *Elders don't let go.*

Many elders, fearing a loss of identity, hold on too long to their family business.

- *Elders don't stay engaged.*

Once they firmly decide they have better things to do with their remaining time, they often say things like, "I want out."

- *Elders don't believe.*

They have a hard time believing that something better could come along than what they've already produced. And they especially don't believe that someone from the next generation might be able to come up with that better thing.

- *Elders don't model effectively.*

Elders who can't let go tend to provide only one example of leadership, mostly bad.

- *Elders resist transition.*

They're fond of quoting statements like, "If it ain't broke, don't fix it."

Note that I called these common errors, not inevitable or universal ones. Many elders have terrific traits, too, including two big ones:

- *Elders love to tell their stories.*

I would strongly advise the younger generation that even if these stories sound like some version of, "I had to walk uphill five miles both ways through the snow to get to school and back," you need to listen to these stories. Honor them. Learn from them.

- *Elders have deep and rugged character forged through struggle.*

The elder generation wants to be valued and respected. Remember that the "good old days" weren't always so good. Struggle and risk were part and parcel of getting this family business off the ground. The elder generation often has a Depression-era mentality (addressed below) that wants to make life better (read *easier*) for the next generation; but in reality, those struggles usually made them and shaped them, particularly their character.

I think it's important to note here that in the next generation's attempt to step up and take initiative, along with the change that will necessarily be a part of transition, next-gen members can give the impression that the elder generation did things the "wrong" way. Change is inevitable, but it doesn't necessarily mean that what came before was wrong.

Before I turn my attention to followers, the next generation, I admit that sometimes it's easier to think of founders and followers as groups with two completely different mind-sets. But followers can adopt a founder mentality. It's important to know, generation by generation, the wiring, temperament, and particular preferences of the person calling the shots.

The Follower Generation

I call the younger generation "the followers" simply because they follow the founders. Note what often characterizes the younger generation:

- *Followers want to be heard.*

Increasingly, these followers do not feel motivated so much by finances as by having a voice and making a difference. And, by the way, the voice they want and the difference they aim for very likely differ from those of the elder generation. The two have different targets.

- *Followers want to avoid the mistakes of their elders.*

They want to learn from the elder generation but not walk down the same blind alleys as their predecessors. A friend says it this way: "The young bucks don't want to pay the 'dumb tax.' They do want to learn from the mistakes of their elders."

- *The younger generation's misperceptions about the elder generation can wreak havoc in a family business.*

These misperceptions often morph into suspicions. Left unchecked, suspicions destroy trust and create resentment. Let me give an example.

Bill, in his midfifties, employs several family members in their late twenties and early thirties. Bill's daughter observes him going off and doing other things—such as personal projects and community service. She can never seem to reach him on his cell phone, and he doesn't bother to listen to his voice mail. She begins to think (actually, she's been thinking this for several years), "He's off doing his own thing. I'm putting in way more hours than I signed on for, and he's taking all the cash out of the company."

Here's the truth: Daughter has no idea what Dad did to give his kids a chance to own a business and carry on the family enterprise. Now, it is true that Daughter's voice needs to be heard. And it is true that what Dad has contributed needs to be honored and respected. But it is also true that, left unchecked, the daughter's suspicions and resentments will not lead to a healthy business environment, let alone a healthy relationship with her dad.

And so we come back again to those two words: *family . . . business.*

A Look at the Generations

It might help us to take a bit of time to observe several distinctive traits about the generations that populated the twentieth and twenty-first centuries in America.

1. World War I, the Roaring Twenties, the Great Depression (1914–1930)

Let's roll the clock back almost a century. The Great Depression gave birth to several mantras:

- "We want to make it better for our children. We don't want them to go through what we went through, often wondering where we'd get our next meal."
- "You can't trust the stock market. The only safe place for your money is the bank."
- "Work hard and it might just pay off. If not, work hard anyway."
- "The Good Book says, 'God helps those who help themselves.'" (The Good Book doesn't actually say any such thing, but the Depression-era generation usually lived as though it did.)

The beliefs and outlooks of this generation generated consequences both positive and negative:

- Because most excess was wiped out in the Great Depression, innovation emerged, leading to the birth of some of America's great companies.
- Out of the country's financial and social trials, people learned to be patient, to persevere, and to have a long-term perspective. Solid character was instilled in many members of that generation.
- Because parents born in the Great Depression wanted to pass on "a better life" to their children, this taught the next generation a form of parenting that, in my opinion, has contributed to a "more is better" mentality. "A better life" therefore translated to more money, more house, more stuff.
- Partly because most folks didn't have any money, that generation learned to keep quiet about both money and feelings. They learned to "do," not to "communicate."

2. World War II and the Builder Generation (1930–1945)

This generation, those born before 1945, had a strong sense of the nuclear family. While some moms of this generation worked outside the home, the bulk of them bore the load when it came to running the home and raising the kids. This generation worked hard to pass along this "better life." They had a kind of hope that the Depression-era folk just didn't have.

Radio was the key technological advancement of the day. Strict discipline was the rule. For the most part, this generation had job security. Many workers stayed loyal to their employers for a lifetime. Large companies provided lifetime income at retirement in the form of pensions. Lots of family businesses appeared, whether farms, manufacturing companies, or mom-and-pop storefronts. Parenting happened, but no one yet thought to teach it.

3. Baby Boomers (1946–1964)

This is my generation (I was born in 1956). While the early baby boomers faced a draft with the real possibility of serving in Vietnam, my slice of baby boomers didn't have to worry about compulsory military service. This removed some fear from our baby boomer psyche, but it also tended to remove some other things: service to our country, the risk of facing death in combat, and seeing clearly whether "I have what it takes."

My generation grew up on TV, even if it was black-and-white and only four channels. My generation enjoyed travel options like none before. Our parents generally made it all about us. It was a no-brainer for many families that the children would go to college. To "make a better life," we were told we *had* to go to college. Some in my generation started businesses or, after college, returned to family businesses, but most of us fell into two categories: you either began climbing the corporate ladder, or you went out to save the world (even the hippies of the sixties often jumped onto the ladder as they moved into their thirties and forties). We sought to know how to "get in touch with ourselves," and we attended parenting classes or at least prenatal classes. For many of us, money bought options, and the more you had, the better it was.

4. Gen X (1965-1980)

Think about this time in history. In America, we saw the end of sending soldiers to Vietnam. We also saw gas rationing, Woodstock, man on the moon, and high interest rates. As we moved through the seventies, interest rates went up and up. Cable TV rose in popularity, and personal computers entered the picture. The "need" to accumulate wealth for one's own retirement became even stronger. As the seventies drew to a close, disco was the rage. The sexual revolution was well underway.

More moms worked, giving birth to a generation of "latch-key kids." The number of single-parent families rose as divorce became increasingly socially accepted. Globalization began to kick in as travel and technology advanced.

5. Gen Y (1980-2000)

The eighties brought us Reaganomics and an explosion of new millionaires in America and around the world as markets opened up with seemingly endless opportunities. We also had to deal with Iran Contra and a variety of political revolutions around the globe. As we moved into the nineties, we saw AIDS emerge as a global health, financial, and political issue. Then we saw "the wall" come down. How scared were we all by the looming threat of Y2K?

Technological advancements and the Internet shrank the world and made a wealth of information instantly available. Many Gen X/Yers and millennials began to believe in a flattened hierarchy of authority ("My opinion is just as valid as yours").

6. Millennials (born since 2000)

This generation is experiencing increasing globalization, immigration issues, and the threats of global warming and terrorism. They will never know a time without iTunes and iPhones, even in the face of the Great Recession. Issues of race relations and tolerance, while often editorialized and plastered on front pages (oops—hardcopy newspapers and magazines are close to casualties in this generation), are often non-issues to millennials. It is assumed (a dangerous word) that everyone thinks alike on these issues.

Studies show that millennials tend to value a sense of autonomy, mastery, and purpose. For them, once they have enough money so that money is no longer a worry and they have enough to pay bills and focus on work, dangling the carrot of more money can work *against* motivation. They would certainly agree with Daniel Pink, who said, "When the profit motive becomes unmoored from the purpose motive, bad things happen."[1] Some are saying that this generation (in America) will be the first to have a decrease in economic wealth since the Great Depression.

Millennials tend to create a "life portfolio." Many have multiple jobs and even start their own businesses. We're finding that they value being able to make a contribution, work that makes a difference, and striking their own proper work/life balance. Maybe the millennials can teach us baby boomers a thing or two.

So What?

By now you're probably wondering, "What does all this have to do with the success of multigenerational family enterprises?" Several things, I believe.

Four or five years ago, I facilitated an off-site company retreat for a business owned by two baby boomers. The owners had grown concerned about their employees' lack of punctuality. They both placed a high value on being on time. Their employees, meanwhile, were mostly Gen Xers, moms and dads who shared parenting responsibilities. When the owners insisted on the priority of punctuality, they got an instant pushback from their employees: "What's it matter if I show up at 9 or 9:15? If you text me at 7:30 p.m. with a question and I'm having drinks with friends, I take time to answer you 'on my time.'"

Do you see the generational differences? Clocking in and clocking out don't matter much to Gen Xers. In a sense, they are *always* on the clock. With technology, they sense that they are constantly connected.

Or consider another example. I call it the Gen X definition of "flextime." Many Gen Xers believe that their time is *their* time. They may take "company" time to tend to family or friend matters, even if the boss thinks they should reserve those errands for "personal" time. At the very least, the boss thinks they should schedule that time off.

(And yes, here I go, making this topic an "us/them" issue. I will address the danger of this kind of thinking in a later chapter.)

During that "time off," the Gen Xers continue to communicate with their colleagues at work. They remain connected. And so they think, "What's the problem?"

I think this mind-set helped to contribute to the acceptance of telecommuting. But things constantly change, don't they? Recently, some companies, including behemoths like Intel, have begun to cut back on telecommuting, as they have seen a decrease in productivity among their telecommuters.

Not just generationally, but particularly between generations, we need to push pause and define what we mean by terms like *time*. Different people and different generations have differing definitions. Likewise, many younger professionals have little interest in owning a firm. They just want "a job."

The theory of social relativity can come into play when we discuss generations and how their perspectives differ. To a fifty-year-old, for example, a year is 2 percent of her lifetime. To a twenty-year-old, that same year is 5 percent of his lifetime.

When families discuss succession, therefore, the younger generation can often have a "How long?" or an "Are we there yet?" mentality. Members of the older generation may well be oblivious to this way of thinking. "I started this," they say, "I'll hold onto it as long as I want." This same mentality can say, "This is *all* mine. You don't *deserve* any of it."

From Mom-and-Pop to Enterprise Thinking

The transition of mom-and-pop operation to small business (enterprise) can often get difficult due to several intergenerational factors. I've seen how the following kind of scenario can exacerbate an already difficult challenge.

Suppose the founder passes on to the next generation a style of working that I call "mom-and-pop" (or the next generation simply mimics the founder). In a mom-and-pop world, we all know where the buck stops. That's all to the good.

Another way to look at this is to compare sole proprietors to teams. The sole proprietor makes unilateral decisions and in one sense answers to no one. In a team setting, team members must consider the opinions of others and must answer to one another.

In a mom-and-pop world, we also tend to create a hierarchy that inhibits growth. If everything flows through Mom and Pop, then others in the organization never really lead or soar. When the next generation blindly follows that model, the business never transforms into a true enterprise.

Mom-and-pop thinking differs in many ways from small business thinking. For one thing, since Mom and Pop have to be aware of everything and are responsible for everything, "I" statements never morph into "we" statements.

Moving from mom-and-pop thinking to enterprise thinking represents a generational shift in the business that requires intentionality. Without such a shift, growth remains stunted, both at the personal level and at the business level. I've seen this happen repeatedly.

When the founder holds onto duties and responsibilities for too long, or when she rules as a benevolent dictator, other staff members and often family members get stuck in a sort of time warp. They become forty-year-olds still wearing diapers. And, believe me, it's tough to potty train a forty-year-old!

When the founder/elder fails to delegate any authority, she also fails to build ownership or share responsibility. When that happens, you see promising managers still running everything by the founder. They never learn how to take appropriate risk, and when the day comes when those long-tenured managers have to learn to think on their own or take appropriate risks, they get a lot of looking over their shoulders. You hear statements in staff meetings like, "I might get in trouble for saying this, but . . ."

And so I wonder: What have they missed out on along the way because their organizations remain stuck in a sort of time warp? Enterprise thinking (when an organization evolves to small business thinking) allows Mom and Pop to take vacations. If enterprise thinking is in place, things might just work out fine when Mom and Pop are away. In fact, (gasp!) they might even work better!

It's Nothing New

A clash of generations isn't anything new. In fact, we can go back thousands of years to the biblical story of Jacob, working for the girl of his dreams, Rachel.

Jacob fell so hard for Rachel that he agreed to work seven years in return for permission to marry her. The story goes, "Jacob served seven years for Rachel, and they seemed to him but a few days because of the love he had for her."[2]

Sounds grand, doesn't it? But the man with whom Jacob struck this bargain, Rachel's father, Laban, didn't see things quite the way Jacob did. When the two men finally parted company after two decades and divided the livestock, Jacob felt he had been fair in what he'd given and what he'd taken. An angry Laban did not agree. Laban said to Jacob, "These women are my daughters, these children are my grandchildren, and these flocks are my flocks—in fact, everything you see is mine."[3]

Generations view differently what they've put in the pot and what they've taken out. It's normal.

I can only see through my eyes. You can only see through your eyes. If both of us see the value of varied perspectives, then we can thrive. If we see only the conflict that these different perspectives bring, however, then we're in for trouble over the long haul.

Certain things are generational from a societal point of view: items like world events, technology, and media. Other things are generational based on where you are in the "family tree" of the family business. Are you first, second, third, or fourth generation? It makes a difference. To prove the point, just ask yourself, "What motivates me?" The fact is that what motivates you and your generation may not motivate me and my fellow baby boomers at all.

The Evolution of a Family Business

Classic family business literature describes the generational evolution of family businesses. It looks something like this:

1. *Founder/sole proprietor*
2. *Sibling partnership*
3. *Cousin consortium*

Is it any wonder that, given the exponentially expanding potential owners, only 3 *percent* of family businesses make it to the fourth generation?

If you take nothing else from this chapter, take this: Generational differences are *real*. Be aware of them. Their preferences and tendencies aren't necessarily right or wrong; they're just different.

"My daddy did it this way, I did it this way, and you'll do it this way," just isn't good enough if you want your business to thrive. Each generation has its own preferred way of doing things—and that's actually a very good thing.

SIX

▼

the roles we play and the hats we wear

I'll never forget a not-too-proud moment many years ago when I helped coach my son's seventh-grade basketball team. One day when he came out of a game, I tore into him. When he pushed back, I yelled, "I'm wearing my Coach hat, not my Dad hat!"

Drew has always been sharp. Immediately he replied, "Then why aren't you getting on other players the way you're getting on me?"

Touché!

That experience taught me that it is of utmost importance to be clear about what "hat" you're wearing when you make comments to other members of your team. And that's true whether the team involves sports or business.

In your business, are you wearing the Dad hat, the Owner hat, or the Boss hat? Are you aware of the various hats you wear and the different roles you play?

Only when we're aware of the roles we play do we have a chance of making headway and not getting stuck. A lack of awareness on the part of the role player and other team members will lead only to a downward spiral.

In this chapter, I want to describe a dozen of the roles that often exist in family businesses. By no means do these roles make up an exhaustive list! I'm always adding to my list and you will too. But I hope that you will recognize some of these roles. Some you've already played, some you are playing, and others you will play. Some roles will better fit other team and family members.

The key thing to remember with all of these roles is this: *Be prepared to be aware!* Don't get caught wearing a derby when you really need a sombrero.

A Dozen Common Roles in Family Business

The Matriarch

I'll bet you can name the matriarch's mantra without anyone even telling you. She says, "Can't we all just _____?"

You filled in the blank, didn't you? "Get along."

Mom wants *peace*. She wants her "babies" to be happy. This role has so many positive aspects to it, but I've also noticed one problematic aspect that shows up, especially when the time comes to talk about the tough stuff in a family business. Because Mom wants everyone to get along, conflict is tough for her. When the lid gets taken off and discovery begins, she can have a tendency to run. She can hijack some of the necessary work needed to uncover real issues and so prevent anyone from addressing those issues in a healthy way. And then what happens to the well-being of the family and the business?

We can look at this role from another angle. Suppose that when multiple generations work together, Mom has customarily served as the holiday hostess and outing organizer. If she doesn't remain aware of the hat she's wearing, she can get in the way of the next-gen family developing its own sense of nuclear family.

Imagine that Mom and Dad invite everyone on a cruise. All the kids come along, and one of them brings his own kids. Mom assumes (uh-oh, that word again) that everyone will always eat as a group and do all the excursions together. But the next-gen family wants to bond one day by doing a cruise excursion on their own. If no one communicates about this, Mom can end up feeling hurt and even disrespected. On the other hand, if all the kids just keep quiet and comply with Mom's wishes, then the next-gen nuclear family can develop strong feelings of resentment.

The Scapegoat

Does someone in your family consistently end up being the fall guy? Does one person seem like easy pickings when things go wrong? If your family has a history of substance abuse, often the abuser becomes the scapegoat. Be careful here! It's easy to dump undeserved blame on the scapegoat.

As our kids grew up, especially in their younger years, Lyn and I often had a hard time figuring out which of them had messed up. One time, one of them wrote in crayon on a wall. We agreed that unless one of them fessed up, we wouldn't do the fun thing we had announced we would do. We waited and waited. Finally, Drew, two years his sister's junior, said, "Mom and Dad, I did it." He took the blame and received the punishment and then we all went and had ice cream. A long time later, Drew and I were talking when somehow this incident came up. "Yeah," Drew admitted, "I said I did it, but I didn't. I just wanted to go get ice cream."

Drew often became the household scapegoat. I wonder, how many times without cause?

The Golden Child

I don't believe most parents set out to play favorites. "Don't make me pick my favorite child," nearly all parents think, even if they never say it out loud. Here's another area where we can find ourselves in the ditch before we know it.

If you find yourself in a situation where you sense preferential treatment is taking place, talk about it. "Johnny can do no wrong." "Susie hung the moon." Those kinds of statements create resentment against Johnny and Susie and can create an unbearable load for Johnny and Susie to bear, especially among their siblings.

The Prodigal Child

You probably remember the classic story told in the fifteenth chapter of the gospel of Luke called the parable of the prodigal son. A younger son asks Dad for his inheritance, goes off and squanders it, and returns home with his tail between his legs. Dad welcomes him back and throws a big party, acting as though his son has come back from the dead.

Let's modernize the tale. Parents find out that one of their kids has a drug problem. The addict heads off in Mom's new Beemer, wrecks it, gets thrown in jail for drunk driving, goes into rehab, and returns home, only to get a corner office at the newly remodeled building the family business has just occupied. During his rehab at an out-of-state treatment center (that looks a lot like a spa), Mom and Dad vacationed nearby while the two other siblings not only kept the business running but also supervised the remodeling of the building. Does that sound a little more familiar?

Big Bird

A guy at the gym where I exercise is a second-generation business owner. It seems to me that while he's shown up for work for decades, he has benefited mightily from his dad's hard work. Dad built a sort of "nest" for him—and birds are meant to fly when they get big. They're not supposed to stay in the nest.

I often hear things from this guy that don't sound terribly mature. They frequently prompt me to think, "This guy hasn't grown up." Not very generous on my part, I know. But the story illustrates my point.

Birds are meant to leave the nest, flap their wings, and fly. Sometimes parents, with the best of intentions, clip their kids' wings by letting them stay in the nest for far too long.

The Old Soul

In stark contrast to Big Bird is the Old Soul. You know these people the moment you meet them.

When the son of a former neighbor was maybe nine years old, we got a call in the middle of the night from our neighbors telling us they were at the hospital with their son, who had just been diagnosed with an inoperable tumor. My wife immediately responded, "We have to go be with them!" And so we left for the hospital.

Eventually doctors did operate, extracting a tumor from this boy's spine. During the procedure, they took out chunks of each vertebra. As he recovered, he endured a sort of imposed scoliosis, which led to all sorts of problems. A few years later, our neighbor took an annual bike trip with a youth group. His son joined him, although he had just undergone a round of chemo, so he wasn't feeling too hot. After one long, grueling day in the saddle, everyone gathered around the campfire, including a bunch of healthy (though not necessarily fit) teenagers, complaining about their aches and pains—and there sat my neighbor's son, just glad to be there. My neighbor told me, "He's become our little Yoda."

That boy is an Old Soul.

Listen to the Old Souls in your family and in your business! You have much to learn from them.

Do you know the key difference between Big Bird and the Old Soul? It comes down to one word: *adversity*. In his book *The Me I Want to Be*, John Ortberg writes:

> Imagine you have a child and you are handed a script of her entire life laid out before you. Better yet, you are given an eraser and five minutes to edit out whatever you want. You read that she will have a learning disability in grade school. . . . After high school she will get into the college she wanted to attend, but while there she will lose a leg in a car crash. Following that, she will go through a difficult depression. A few years later she will get a great job, then lose that job in an economic downturn. She will get married, but then go through the grief of separation.
>
> With this script of your child's life before you and five minutes to edit it, what would you erase? That is the question psychologist Jonathan Haidt asked in this hypothetical exercise. Wouldn't you want to take out all the stuff that would cause them pain? We live in a generation of "helicopter parents" who constantly swoop in to their children's lives to make sure no one is mistreating them and that they experience one unobstructed success after another in school, sports, and relationships.

Whoa! If you could wave a wand and erase every failure, disappointment, and suffering, are you sure it would be a good idea? Would that enable your children to grow into the best version of themselves? Is it possible that in some way people actually need adversity and setbacks—maybe even something like trauma—to reach the fullest level of development and growth? Paul believed that as we live in the flow of the Spirit, suffering can lead to growth. Suffering can actually produce more flourishing people.[1]

Who are the Old Souls in your family business? What sort of adversity has made them into the people they are? How could your business benefit from paying closer attention to their observations and perspectives?

The Leader

Who is the real Leader in your family business? I'm not talking about an official leadership role. We all lead to some degree, even if the only thing we lead is our own life. I have in mind here "the Big-L" Leader. This kind of leadership is innate, a gift. The Leader sees things that others don't see. This Leader has duck feathers—stuff that would destroy others just rolls off her back.

I used to be this kind of Leader on the basketball court. If there were three seconds left and we were tied, I wanted the last shot. If time had expired and my team was down one, I wanted the ball in my hands, shooting two free throws. Leaders thrive under pressure. But this vision can be both a blessing and a curse.

Years later, when I watched my kids play ball, I couldn't turn off what I saw. While I had a choice about what to do with what I saw, I didn't often win that battle. I yelled at the refs a lot.

At times, Leaders need to bridle what they see. Not all of what a Leader sees is fit for public consumption! Who are the real Leaders in your organization? Identify them and let them lead. Be aware, though, that Big-L Leaders leave a wake behind them. Others often have to clean up the debris in their wake.

The Risk Manager

Risk Managers are glass-half-empty people. "Can we afford to do that? I'm not sure we should be taking that on right now." Risk Managers often make these kinds of statements, and so they are a great yin to the Big-L Leader's yang. Risk Managers keep Big-L Leaders out of jail.

With rare exceptions, however, Risk Managers in the leadership chair of a business or organization will never capture the full growth potential of that business or organization. I often liken the Risk Manager to a trustee. What is the trustee's mandate? "Don't lose whatever has been entrusted to you."

But wait! Risk Managers rarely think about what *could* be. They typically focus on what might go wrong, not on what could go spectacularly well. At seasons in the life of a family business, a Risk Manager might be a more appropriate CEO than a Big-L Leader. Companies with a monopoly in a market or organizations serving a government mandate, for example, can competently be led by Risk Managers. But businesses that want and need to grow in new areas usually need someone other than a Risk Manager in the captain's chair.

The New Testament records a parable about a man we might characterize as a Risk Manager. In the parable of the talents, one man operated entirely with the focus, "Don't lose what you've been given"—and in the story, he gets judged harshly for it. When the time comes for him to explain what he's done with his master's money, he replies, "I knew that you are a hard man . . . So I was afraid."[2] Fear often drives a Risk Manager—but the Risk Manager's fear-driven view of "the master" seldom inspires him to greatness.

The Crossing Guard

Who holds up the "stop sign" in your family business? Who says, "This conversation is fruitless"? Who says, "You're fighting over nothing. Stop it!"?

In our family, my daughter, Lindsay, is the Crossing Guard. On many occasions when Lyn and I have started a fight over something, we've heard Lindsay say, "This is dumb. Stop fighting! This doesn't even matter."

The Lifeguard

Do you have a "rescuer" in your organization? Someone who regularly jumps in and bails out the guilty party? Or do you have someone who, with the best of intentions, stops a misunderstanding before a conflict arises, even though it's a conflict that needs to happen so it can be mined? If someone makes a habit of coming to the rescue, be aware of the highly demotivating message that this can send to other team members.

The Senior with Senioritis

An associate and I met recently with the members of an intergenerational family business. The transition from one generation to the next has nearly completed. We asked Dad ("Joe," not his real name) how he thought things were progressing. Joe expressed his excitement at getting to the end of the year, when he would finally be "free" to move on to this thing called retirement. My associate said to Joe, "It sounds to me like this is the spring semester of your senior year." The thought immediately popped into my head, "Joe has senioritis." I spoke my thought out loud, and everyone had a good laugh.

Can you remember back to your senior year in high school? For some of us, that's more than four decades ago. It probably wasn't a time of high motivation, was it? We were counting the days until our freedom. We could hardly wait for graduation. Many of us had already decided on college, and our GPAs suffered that final semester.

While such a disengagement might play well for a high school senior, be careful when it comes to "graduating" from your family business. If senioritis sets in, some of the "know how/know who" might be lost to the business forever, never to be recovered.

The Blessing Bestower

Too often I've seen the elder generation be too hard on their kids. The "it's never good enough" perception is hard to live down.

We once worked with a family that had five kids, two of whom worked in the business. Mom and Dad desperately wanted things to work out between the two brothers, but the boys were oil and water and simply didn't get along. Mom and Dad ached at the conflict. At times, they took sides. In the end, a separation had to occur and one son decided to move away. I still hope that his choice to create some space might generate a new perspective for all parties that will one day open the door for reconciliation.

Once he made the decision to leave—even though Mom and Dad questioned his choice and wondered aloud about the real "Why?" of the move—I said, "What he and his wife need now is not your suspicions but your blessing." I had the privilege of sitting in with the four of them and watching Mom and Dad bestow their blessing on their son and daughter-in-law. I felt as though I was standing once again on holy ground.

Our kids need to know we're with them and behind them, that we believe in them. Are there blessings yet to be bestowed in your family?

Where Do You Fit?

You might already be familiar with the three circles below. Where do you fit in the three circles?[3]

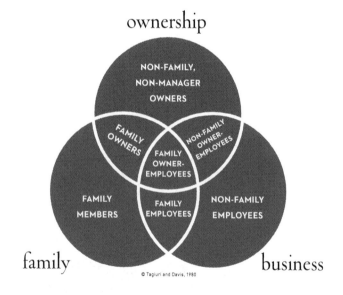

© Tagiuri and Davis, 1980

Take some time to place each of your team members in an appropriate area above. In how many of the sections do your team members fall? Can this help you to see how each of them may have a different perspective in operating the business? How could this change the way you relate to them and work with them?

To Blossom, Be Aware

Without question, the list of roles I've described in this chapter leaves out some of the roles you play in your own family business. Take a look at your own situation and identify the roles you see played there. The key is to be aware of the roles you play and the hats you wear.

To enable your business to fully blossom, you need to identify both the roles to play and the roles to avoid. You simply must identify these roles if you want to build the kind of relationships and communication you desire. Only then will you be able to pursue a healthy, compelling vision for the future of your family and your business.

SEVEN

▼

trust

All of us know that trust is a huge issue in families and businesses. But it's an even bigger issue in family businesses. The challenge is to identify issues related to trust and then face them head on.

Everyone has their own thoughts, conversations, and experiences related to trust. But for the purposes of this brief book, I want to ask you a simple but enormous question:

How big of a deal to you is trust?

Questions, Questions

Here's some food for thought, in the form of questions, as you work through identifying and prioritizing the trust issues you must address over time.

- What impact does trust have on your family business, regardless of whether you make trust a priority to be addressed?

- Do you sense that trust is high in your family? In your business?
- Do you often hear comments like, "I just don't trust her"?
- Are you a trusting person?
- Would others call you trustworthy?
- While we all would say trust is important, would your employees say trust is a value on display in your company?

Trust Is Built Over Time

Trust is built with time and consistency. And while trust is hard to acquire and to build, it's staggeringly easy to lose.

Some say trust is based on character and competence.

Healthy organizations not only exhibit trust, they talk about it. If you hear, "Why don't you trust me?" it's time for some serious sit-down conversation.

Stephen M. R. Covey, Stephen Covey's son, wrote a powerful book titled *The Speed of Trust: The One Thing That Changes Everything*. In a nutshell, Covey said that if trust is high in an organization, cost goes down and things get done more quickly. Conversely, said Covey, when trust is low, things slow down and costs rise.

Covey described something he called, "The Roddick Choice." In an Italian tennis tournament, Andy Roddick had a match point, when, to his own detriment, he told the judge a ball hit by his opponent was in when the judge had ruled it out. He went on to lose the match. Going forward, will judges listen to Roddick's challenges? Yes, because he built trust.[1]

Later in the book, Covey listed thirteen behaviors that build trust:

1. Straight talk—talk straight—speak truth in love
2. Show respect
3. Create transparency
4. Right wrongs
5. Show loyalty
6. Deliver results
7. Get better
8. Confront reality—discuss the "undiscussable"
9. Clarify expectations
10. Practice accountability
11. Listen first
12. Keep commitments
13. Extend trust—use good judgment—don't be gullible or overly suspicious[2]

One mom and dad went to Europe for six months. Previously when they went away, they regularly checked in. They didn't want to micromanage from a distance, but they did try to manage from a distance. On this trip, they intentionally did not check in at all. And surprise of all surprises, thing went remarkably well in their absence.

What do you think that communicated to the next-gen management group? "We believe in you. We trust you. You have what it takes."

The A-Frame of Trust

Luke Naismith, in a blog titled "Knowledge Futures," offered what he called the "A-Frame of Trust":

a-frame of trust

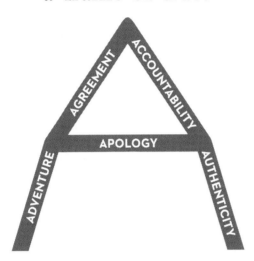

Let me comment on each of the five pieces of scaffolding, especially as it relates to family businesses.

Agreement: Agreement isn't the same thing as consensus. When we have a management meeting behind closed doors, we invite disagreement; we want to get it all out on the table. But at some point, we as a management team will have to come out from behind the closed doors. And once we do, we must present to the rest of the team a united front. Getting to that kind of agreement takes work.

Accountability: We've engaged clients in a simple exercise: "Your homework is to write down one way you'd like to raise your personal bar during the next twelve months." At the next team meeting, everyone tells the group what they wrote down. Now everyone's gone public, and that invites team members to hold each other accountable to how each of them wants to improve.

Apology: Lyn and I found that one of the best ways to build the greatest level of trust with our kids was by confessing our wrongdoings. Leaders who apologize build trust.

Adventure: I like to think of this as risk-taking. Andy Crouch says, "True flourishing is only found on the far side of risk."[3]

Authenticity: Vulnerability leads to believability when it starts with the leader.

The A-frame provides the scaffolding of this "home" we want to live in, a home characterized by an atmosphere of trust.[4]

What is at risk if we don't address trust as a critical issue? While trust is earned through time and consistency, trust also must be extended. And that's risky business.

Remember the mom and dad who went away for an extended time without meddling with things back home? That's good—but a word of caution here. Don't burn up upon re-entry! You can quickly burn up any trust you've built during your absence if, when you return, you immediately go back to doing things as you did before you left.

Scaling the Wall of Trust

"Trust can't be hot-wired," warned Brené Brown in *Rising Strong*.[5] In fact, trust is a very fragile thing. You have to handle it with care. I've told clients that gaining trust is like scaling a vertical rock wall. Slowly you pound a hook into the rock face. You inch your way up. It's a slow process, and the consequences of a fall are grave.

It's that way with trust. If you "fall" or "break," the consequences are grave.

Rock climbers often take mountain guides with them. They invest in training and they plan. They don't take the climb lightly.

Should it be any different with you and your team as together you scale the wall of trust?

Some of the ropes courses and other team-oriented exercises designed to build trust may seem a bit worn-out, but don't neglect opportunities like this. Any time you invest in your team, they know it. You create buy-in, and buy-in builds trust.

So intentionally take time (paid time for employees) to go off-site for retreats and other activities. You may not think these things are productive, but creating space to get to know team members on a deeper level will reap huge dividends in your team members' lives and in your business. You will be amazed at the creativity that emerges when you trust your people with this kind of time and space.

When Trust Erodes

Inevitably, you *will* suffer breakdowns in trust. When you do, address them in a timely way. Be specific. Involve all interested parties.

The next time you sense trust eroding, try this. First, stop. Ask several things of the person with whom you're having the trust issue:

- "What did you hear me say?"
- "What do you think I meant?"
- "How did that make you feel?"

Practice this. Then watch as it starts to help you climb back up that sheer rock wall of trust.

Do the Hard Work

Scaling this rock wall of trust is risky. And often our fears keep us from persevering in scaling the trust wall.

We must commit to the hard work anyway. "We can do the hard work of facing a problem and making the necessary changes to resolve it, and then we will enjoy the easy road of having things right," writes Dr. Henry Cloud in *Integrity*. "But the hard comes first and must be endured. Or, we can take the easy route first and avoid fixing a problem. Then, as sure as the sun will come up tomorrow, the hard life will follow. And it will last a lot longer and will be a lot harder than if we had chosen the hard way first."[6]

Choosing the hard way is choosing to scale this vertical, risky wall of trust. The hard work must come first. And then comes the easier road of having things right.

EIGHT

▼

finances

People can say that money doesn't matter, but what exactly do they mean? The truth is, finances are a big deal to everybody. My wife and I recently sat down over lunch with a younger associate and his wife. During our time together, I had a real *aha* moment. We get together periodically with this couple to help practice some of what we covered in chapter 4 about voice and vote. We want to keep the lines of communication open and avoid relational drift.

As we talked about money and how to work through issues of ownership and income in a small business, Lyn said, "It's not about the money." She meant that she doesn't feel too excited at this stage of our lives about taking big financial risks for some possible big gain in equity. She wants to enjoy life and be generous while we're alive. Income is therefore more important to her than equity.

To our young associate, the "It's not about the money" statement applies to income. His income took a big leap this past year. As he explained that he and his wife have chosen their lifestyle and that this jump in income wouldn't change their lifestyle choice, the *aha* hit me. The statement "It's not about the money" has a different meaning for him than it does for Lyn. For him, it's not about the income, while for Lyn, it's not about the equity. This understanding wouldn't have occurred had we not slowed down and taken the time to listen to each other.

The incident reminds me that conversations about money in a family business context require both time and intentionality.

Watch Out for Assumptions

Assumptions can kill us here too. Try on these common ones:

- "I just assumed you were giving me the stock in the company."
- "I just assumed you'd saved for retirement and at age sixty-five were going to live off of your retirement savings, Social Security, and your other investments."
- "I just assumed, since we never talked about it, that you were going to sell the business to someone else."
- "I just assumed that as time went on, our incomes would become similar."
- "I just assumed that since I'd always been paid for my extra hours, I would continue to get overtime pay with this new position."
- "I just assumed Mom and Dad were leaving the estate equally to us three kids."

All these assumptions relate to personal income and assets. But what about assumptions regarding the business itself? Have you had these kinds of discussions?

- "Do we borrow money? If so, under what circumstances?"
- "What happens to profits? Do we reinvest them or pay them out as bonuses and/or dividends?"
- "Should we have a retirement plan? Should the company contribute to it?"
- "What 'personal expenses' should/does the company pay?"
- "How do we decide whether to move or build a facility? Or expand?"
- "Should the business own the real estate on which it operates?"
- "How big is big enough?"
- "Who can own stock in the company?"
- "How do we make financial decisions?"
- "Are employed family members paid the same as others who hold the same position? Are they underpaid? Are they overpaid (is there a 'family factor' in the way their compensation is determined)?"
- "What about charity and generosity—toward family, employees, and charitable organizations?"
- "Do we have a family philosophy about money and possessions?"

When families and businesses don't address these issues, problems inevitably result. Assumptions become conclusions, misunderstanding mounts, unnecessary conflict erupts, resentment stews, relationships rupture, and anger boils over. Unexamined and undiscussed assumptions never lead to anything good.

Avoid the Pitfalls

Why not address these topics head-on? When you refuse to do so, you choose a path fraught with pitfalls and peril.

Talking about money, particularly among family members, used to be taboo. That's not so much the case anymore. Let me encourage you to be intentional about discussing money with both your family members and your business team. It's helpful to understand your own history of money, particularly as it was (or wasn't) discussed in your family of origin.

Believe that change is possible, both for you and for others. Over time, people *can* change their perceptions about money. And that, over time, can change their experience of life.

NINE

▼

this thing called the business

As you keep a careful eye on the issues we've already discussed, who's watching out for this entity known as "the business"? It, too, has a life. And we need to treat it as a key player when we have our conversations.

I recently spoke to a class about the life of a business. Most founders feel as though they've birthed a child, changed its diapers, taught it to walk and talk . . . and now this child is ready to leave the nest? Too often, the founder continues to treat the business as his child and can't believe that this child could survive on its own. During my presentation, one attendee said, "Yeah, sometimes it's his favorite child." Ouch! While I've said the business has a life of its own, be careful that it doesn't become more important than your own family.

Isn't It Obvious?

While it might seem odd to say that you must make the business itself a priority, I know from experience that a lot of business owners get caught up in spending all their time working *in* their business and virtually no time working *on* their business. Does that statement characterize you? If it does, then I contend that you are *not* making your business a priority. At least, you haven't made it the right priority.

Another indicator that something has gone wrong is the workaholic tendency of so many small business owners. They *love* their work. They get consumed by it and other priorities suffer, including the priority of the business.

If neglected, the business might still survive ... but will it thrive? Michael Gerber in his book *The E-Myth Revisited* writes, "If your business depends on you, you don't own a business—you have a job. And it's the worst job in the world because you're working for a lunatic!"[1] To see whether you're working for a lunatic, ask yourself a few questions:

- "If I died tonight, could someone step in and run the show?"
- "Does my family know they'd be taken care of if something happened to me?"
- "Do I have a team made up of the right people ready to face the challenges and take hold of the opportunities in front of us?"
- "Is this the place people in our community want to work?"
- "Am I beginning to let go of what I need to let go of?"
- "Do we have the right team of advisors in place? For me? For the next generation?"

- "Do we have a thoroughly thought-out shareholder agreement?"
- "In our rush to get things done and 'in order,' are we guilty with our documents (as one business consultant says) of *hardwiring dysfunction for generations*?"

It's Up to You

Remember the three questions from the end of chapter 2: The Value Question, The Generation Question, and The Legacy Question. Failing to address these questions makes a significant statement regarding what kind of priority you are placing on "the business."

As I close this part of the book, remember that it's up to you to prioritize the issues you must address once you've clarified them. You can't tackle them all at once. Identification pinpoints them and keeps them on your radar, while prioritization moves certain issues to the front of the queue.

For whatever reason, sometimes a founder will start multiple businesses to accommodate all of her children. While the kids spend all their time on "their" individual businesses, it can be difficult to think about the whole team in the larger business, the parent company. But who's looking out for the whole operation? Who's taking care of Team Number One?

Who's looking out for the whole operation in *your* business?

- part three -

RESOLVE

WORK TOWARD
SHARED SOLUTIONS

TEN

▼

meetings

I've done a number of family meetings in which Mom and Dad came to the meeting with fear and trepidation, wondering what the kids would say. Before one meeting where the whole family came together, we first had individual meetings with Mom and her kids. When it came time for the "big" meeting, Mom audibly worried about what might happen.

"Don't worry," I told her, "these always turn out better than you expect." Sure enough, that day Mom received all kinds of affirmation from her kids. She heard positive things that she'd never before heard from them. There were tears, there was laughter. To watch the weaving and repairing of relationships in real time—who wouldn't want to be part of a meeting like that?

Three Kinds of Meetings

A friend recently suggested that all effective leaders should define what kind of meeting or conversation will take place. Meetings come in three basic varieties:

1. *Command Meeting*: "I'm going to tell you what I've decided we're going to do." (These meetings should be short.)
2. *Consultative Meeting*: "I'm still going to make the decision, but I want your input."
3. *Consensus Meeting*: "I want us to discuss this and reach a consensus on our decision and course of action."

Clarifying what kind of meeting you're going to have can make all the difference. It helps frame participants' expectations. Unmet expectations may not be the root of all evil, but they are the root of a ton of anxiety.

Before you make any decision that impacts a significant number of your people, seek out the input of all involved parties. I've found that most employees don't feel they need to be a part of every decision, even the ones impacting them. What they do want is to be heard.

A team member in one client's company got rubbed the wrong way when he didn't get invited to a meeting called to discuss layoffs. It angered him that he didn't get an invitation to the conversation.

I counseled the team to use this phrase: "I'm not including you in this conversation because I don't want to waste your time. We are not making any decisions at the meeting."

I think it helps everyone to make a clear distinction between *discussion* and *decision*. Practice this and you will avoid some resentment later.

Meeting Suggestions

Let me suggest a few key things to keep in mind as you schedule and prepare to run your meetings.

Who runs the meeting?

Let me suggest that you rotate facilitation, or at least discuss the idea. Ask yourself, "What happens when I am in charge of a meeting?" If you're like most people, you are definitely more engaged when you lead. So what do you think would happen if you rotated that responsibility? The practice will build engagement in all team members over time.

How should we record what happens?

Sometime before the meeting is to take place, ask yourself three important questions:

1. Do we want a way for team members to make agenda suggestions ahead of time?
2. Would it help to send out agendas ahead of time?
3. Do we want to circulate meeting notes after the meeting?

Ask whoever plays the role of "scribe" to take and then circulate the meeting notes. Remind these scribes that they are trying to capture not only the words but also the meaning behind the words. An ancillary benefit of circulating meeting notes is that you'll already have a good start on the next meeting's agenda.

How often should we meet?

Corporations hold annual meetings. Some boards meet quarterly. I like to meet monthly with my clients. Too much drift can occur if the meetings don't occur frequently enough.

As a rule of thumb, the closer the business or the personal relationship, the more frequent the meetings should be. Build momentum early by meeting more frequently. You can always decrease the frequency.

Where should we hold the meetings?

Some meetings can occur in the bull pen, the break room, or on the floor of the operation. Some meetings must happen behind closed doors. But be careful with closed-door meetings! Define for all observers what "closed door" means, or assumptions will run wild.

Some meetings need to occur off-site. Off-campus meetings usually involve fewer interruptions and bring more focus. Too many off-sites, however, can slow momentum, and I've seen a bit of the "when the cat's away . . ." phenomenon take place if your team leaves too often.

Why meet at all?

Sometimes you'll hear, "Why do we even need to meet?" I like to respond like this: "Important things inevitably come up when we get together. Something crucial bubbles to the surface and we can address it. If we don't get together and talk about these things, they tend to get swept under the carpet. Given enough time, the pile under the carpet gets big. Then the lights go out and someone trips over the pile under the carpet and they get hurt."

Who wants that?

What Kind of Meetings?

The word *meetings* is a pretty big and generic term. Let's get more specific about the kinds of meetings you might consider holding.

- Daily check-ins (These might be informal and last only a few minutes.)
- Weekly management (What's on the list for this week?)
- Shareholder meetings

- Next-gen meetings (How can I encourage them to spread their wings?)
- Off-site strategic planning
- Overnight retreats
- Annual retreats
- Family meetings (These could be of the Sunday dinner variety or of the annual retreat variety.)

While not every person on your team has to be involved in every meeting, if you are not intentional about regularly scheduling meetings, communication will inevitably break down, leading to erosion of relationships. That can lead to death by team. I'd rather endure some form of death by meeting (to borrow Patrick Lencioni's memorable phrase) than death by team.[2]

Don't Kill Your People

Do you just *love* to attend meetings? I doubt you do, if you're a normal human being. Many meetings feel like death.

But since meetings are often necessary, make up your mind now to design and have the best kinds of meetings, the kind that don't kill your people. In fact, take the time to describe the kind of meeting you would *like* to attend. What does it look like? Write down a few of its characteristics:

_____
_____
_____

Now, hold *those* kinds of meetings. Don't have unnecessary meetings, but by all means have as many necessary meetings as required. And pray for the wisdom to know what is a "necessary meeting"!

ELEVEN

communication

> Rarely can a response make something better.
> What makes something better is connection.
> —Brené Brown[1]

What would the world be like if we all thought before we spoke? How might things improve if the things needing to be spoken were spoken and the things better left unspoken remained unsaid? Could a timely paraphrase of the Serenity Prayer apply here?

God, grant me the courage to speak what needs to be spoken, the restraint to bite my tongue when I should remain silent, and the wisdom to know the difference.

"But Mark," someone says, "should we really have to keep *that* tight a rein on what we say? Do we all need courage to say what we need to say or to stifle ourselves when we ought to keep quiet?" In short, yes.

In life, some things are better left unsaid. More often, however, some things don't get said that ought to be said. We turn now to these kinds of conversations.

Nothing Good Happens

I doubt any of us needs to strain our brain to come up with a handful of things we wish we'd never said. I can think of many foolish things I've said to Lyn over the years. Once I cross an invisible line in my verbal jousting with my wife, my lizard brain tends to kick in and the venom comes out. Nothing good happens. It reminds me of something we say to our kids about curfews: "Nothing good happens after midnight." When I open my mouth "after midnight" during a heated conflict, *nothing good happens*. But I can't take back what I've said.

I also wonder, though, about the words that I wish I *had* spoken but lacked the courage to speak. How many times have I failed to speak up when I knew I should say something? How often have I kept quiet out of fear of possible repercussions or of what others might think?

When you find yourself in a situation where you think you maybe should speak up, ask yourself, "What's at stake?"

What's at stake if you say what you're thinking about saying?

What's at stake if you don't speak up?

And then ask yourself, "What conversations should be taking place here?" These conversations may benefit the team, a family, or a team member. Or maybe they would be just for your own good. But they really need to happen. The life of Lance Armstrong strongly reinforces this conviction for me.

Break a Secret, Win Your Freedom

Even if you have never followed the Tour de France bike race, you have probably heard of Lance Armstrong, an American cyclist who won seven tours before getting stripped of all his titles. Before the scandal broke, he ascended to heights no one had ever attained in the sport. To make his accomplishment even more impressive, he won all seven championships after beating cancer.

After years of denying that he used performance-enhancing substances, Lance finally visited Oprah's "confession booth" and spilled the beans. As I watched the interview, it struck me that I might have just witnessed the start of a new race for Lance—a race for his freedom.

In the end, once the word got out, the jig was up, and Lance was the only one left trapped in the lie. When he finally confessed his "secret" (not much of one by then), the secret lost its power over him. His freedom was at stake and probably a lot more. He won his freedom . . . but it cost him millions.

I hope Lance can now become a role model to his kids. The false image that he once tried so hard to show to the world reminded me of the famous scene in the classic movie *The Wizard of Oz*. Once Toto pulled back the curtain, the world saw something very different from a powerful wizard.

Couldn't Lance's coming clean, in the end, be part of what it means to become a true role model? Lance's crucial conversation with Oprah definitely played a critical role in helping him make a change for the better.

Crucial Conversations

What constitutes a crucial conversation? If you, your family, or your business faces some mission-critical element that might get missed without having a difficult conversation—or more positively, if you could gain something beneficial by having that discussion—then you need the courage to pursue that conversation. It's crucial.

Consider a few examples of when the stakes rise high enough

that you absolutely must have that discussion. You need to have these crucial conversations whenever you find yourself facing questions like these:

- What should we do with these game-changing ideas and innovations?
- How can we handle interpersonal conflicts that put our relationships at risk or a highly functioning team in jeopardy?
- Should the kids work somewhere else before working in the family business?
- How much of an inheritance is enough?
- Who should lead the next generation in our family business?
- What will bring the kids together once Mom and Dad are gone?
- How can we honor the older generation's value even as their productivity declines?
- What would it look like for you to jump into the deep end of the pool right now? What sort of courage would it take to get you to jump?

What crucial conversations do you need to have *right now* in your own family business? What "secrets" are keeping you from the kind of freedom that would allow both you and your company to soar? What would it take to have these crucial conversations?

Fundamentals of Communication

When you pay attention to and put into practice a few basic fundamentals of communication, you will develop a culture that invites crucial conversations. And when you pursue those conversations, you make it possible for all stakeholders to win.

1. Learn to listen more effectively.

Approach some individuals who know you well and ask them, "Am I a good listener?" If the answer is no, then vow to make a change. Become a disciplined learner. Stephen Covey says, "Most people do not listen with the intent to understand; they listen with the intent to reply."[2]

Learn to practice "deferred listening." Understand that there are some things I can't hear from you right now. If I grow in my ability to listen well and if some of my defensive walls come down, then later you may be able to tell me some things that will have great value down the road. Think of it as compound interest on skillful listening.

2. Deal with blind spots.

We all have blind spots. In the book *Thinking, Fast and Slow*, Daniel Kahneman writes, "We can be blind to the obvious and we are also blind to our blindness."[3] The only way we begin to recognize our blind spots is by seeing ourselves through the eyes of others. So again, find some trusted individuals who know you well and who have the courage to tell you the brutal truth. Ask them, "Am I a person of control or a person of influence?"

It's human nature (and *so* much easier) to talk *about* people rather than *with* people. Many of us do this regularly without even thinking about it. But if leadership falls into this trap, the blind start leading the blind. Fight against this! In your communication with your family and in your business, make the following a part of your practice:

- Talk *with* individuals, not *about* them.
- Push conversations back in the direction from which they came. When someone comes to you and starts talking *about* someone, ask them, "Have you talked with this person about this?" It's a simple way to build this muscle.

3. Ask better questions.

Improve the kinds of questions you are willing to ask and answer. Consider a few great questions:

- Who is the authority in my life?
- Am I open to constructive criticism?
- Is it my way or the highway?
- If you knew you had complete amnesty, that this was a safe place to raise any and every topic, what would you want to discuss right now?
- How am I standing in the way of what this company could become?
- If you had unlimited resources and opportunity, what would you like to see our business become?
- What might we miss out on if we stop talking?
- What kind of information do I seek out? What do I hold onto? What do I do with the information?

4. Recognize there's always another crucial conversation.

We are never "done" with crucial conversations. They need to keep happening. I once helped a family business through conflict and then through a transition that allowed one family member to buy out the interest of another family member. Even though the business part of the family business seemed to have ended, it hadn't. A parent died and an estate had to be settled. Some real estate had to be divided, and since the siblings had separated as business partners, they didn't want to continue as investment business partners. So they tried to fairly negotiate the inherited assets.

It looked as if we were heading down the track of appraisals (and often the one who doesn't order the original appraisal judges the appraisal as unfair, and so ends up ordering another one so that the parties can meet somewhere in the middle). It looked as though the two were going to continue spending money, money, money... and for what? We looked at swapping some houses, but that still didn't look fair. The same patterns of conflict we had seen in the family business began to reappear. I suggested mediation.

We had a meeting with the siblings and their spouses. At first it looked as though we were heading into another impasse, but as we kept talking, eventually a new way emerged.

One of the siblings communicated in a more emotional way than the other. The less emotional one wanted her sibling to have the property and said, "If I had a cash offer on it tomorrow, I'd be sick to my stomach." They were so close to a deal! They kept talking, and finally we found a way to frame a solution where both could live with the outcome.

When relationship is at stake, money often does (and usually should) take a backseat. The moral of the story: *keep talking!* If we don't, we force ourselves into a voting booth and end up framing the decision as win/lose, which for a team always ends up lose/lose. So keep talking! Sometimes a win/win emerges. If we keep talking, eventually we'll get somewhere. We'll uncover new ways to look at things and develop new ideas.

"Never believe somebody who says there are only two ways to think about an issue," said author Donald Miller. "Consumers see two doors. Creators make new ones."[4]

5. A few odds and ends

- Try speaking about conflict resolution. Speak of the mitigation of conflict.
- Remember that a request is not a demand. If you're asked a yes-or-no question, no should be an acceptable answer.
- Bring to mind the acronym WAIT: Why Am I Talking?
- Reserve e-mail for announcing something or memorializing a conversation. If you need dialogue, sit down and talk face-to-face... today, more than ever.
- If you want to bring up an issue with a team member, ask, "Is now a good time?" If it isn't, ask, "Okay, when might be a good time?"

Whatever You Do, Stay Engaged

As we strive to communicate more effectively with one another, we all know we will uncover land mines along the way. That's unavoidable. What we can't afford to do is bury new ones intentionally.

In her wonderful book *Daring Greatly*, Brené Brown speaks frequently of staying engaged. "Are you engaged?" she asks. "Are you paying attention? If so, plan to make lots of mistakes and bad decisions."

In her inimitable style, Brown writes about disruptive engagement: "Make no mistake: honest conversations about vulnerability and shame are disruptive. The reason that we're not having these conversations in our organizations is that they shine light in dark corners... We all want to dare greatly. If you give us a glimpse into that possibility, we'll hold on to it as our vision. It can't be taken away." A bit later she writes, "When we're disengaged, we don't show up, we don't contribute, and we stop caring."[5]

I doubt that's where any of us want to end up—somewhere else emotionally, not contributing, and not caring about any of it. Keeping the lines of communication open and active goes a long way toward people showing up, contributing, and caring deeply about everything.

We can't agree about everything. We can agree about some things. Let's focus on what we can agree upon.

Communication Killers

In my experience, people shut down communication in three main ways: speed, volume, and emotion. Let's take a brief look at all three.

1. Speed

It's not that someone who talks fast is bad. The problem occurs when the speed picks up and the listener struggles to follow. If it does, you can try to slow down the communication by using a technique called "mirroring." Deliberately slow your own speech and see if the other party picks up on your change of speed and then mirrors it. If so, you're back on track. If not, get ready for a derailment.

2. Volume

As with speed, loud isn't always bad; but if the church mouse roars like a lion, then something inside him is hurting. And if the lion continues roaring, he will eventually hunt down and consume his prey.

3. Emotion

Emotion is a tough one for me. I know I could use a higher EQ ("Emotion Quotient," analogous to IQ, Intelligence Quotient).

Most women have much higher EQs than do men. Some of us who aren't emotionally wired to maturity can therefore feel tempted to devalue whatever gets said with emotion. This isn't playing fair. If the emotional intensity ramps up and stays up, however, know that you are headed into a dark tunnel.

You can try to change the communication dynamic by mirroring or intentionally dialing down the rising emotions. If that works, yippee! But if it doesn't, it's probably "after midnight," when nothing good is going to happen. Time for a break! Walk away respectfully.

Pause and Look Back

Stephen M. R. Covey says we must learn to talk straight in a culture of spin.[6] Pursue crucial conversations with all of your mind, heart, will, and strength. Much is at stake. You won't regret it.

And when communication becomes difficult or even painful—as it inevitably will at times—it can help to take a trip down memory lane. How far have you come already? What good memories of family and business could you have "pop up" on your desktop when times get tough?

Keep a "cloudy day" reading file. Even if it isn't Thanksgiving, periodically make a new thanksgiving list. Tell yourself that, just maybe, "We have a good thing here. Let's not screw it up."

TWELVE

transitions

> Give me the strength to die well.
> —William Wallace, just before his execution
> (as played by Mel Gibson in Braveheart)

Transition is not the same thing as change. So said William Bridges in his groundbreaking work *Transitions*.

Change happens daily as I change clothes, change the sheets on the bed, or even change jobs. Transition typically occurs over an extended period of time. Divorce is a good example. A court's decree may legally finalize the end of a marriage, but divorce doesn't start there, and it certainly doesn't end there. Ask any child whose parents have divorced when they or their parents "got over it." You'll probably get a roll of the eyes. In my experience, few people get over divorces. And that illustrates for me the major premise of Bridges' book:

Every transition begins with an ending.[1]

Bridges addressed three stages of transition: an ending, a neutral zone, and a new beginning. In a white paper called "Getting

Them through the Wilderness," he equated these stages with the experience of the ancient Israelites as they left Egyptian slavery. He called the "ending" stage leaving Egypt, the "neutral zone" the wilderness, and the "new beginning" the Promised Land.[2] When I refer my clients to this white paper, they immediately tend to grasp what Bridges meant about the stages of transition. They have a clear understanding of the necessity of leaving the old behind and allowing some real changes to take place if they are to arrive at their promising future. (They especially like it when I tell them this process doesn't have to take forty years.)

Bridges insisted that we cannot take these transition stages out of order. Some people never truly get over a divorce, for example, because their marriage never truly ended. The court papers may say it did, but the heart says otherwise.

When we don't transition well, we get stuck. And the mud we get stuck in affects others. Either they get mud splattered on them or they end up stuck in our mud. "That's not fair!" you say. True enough. But that's life.

And it's true in family business too.

Who Wants to Be a Grumpy Old Man?

Whenever a company makes a new hire, we could call the hire a transaction. The employee now gets a paycheck from a source different than before. This is change. But what is the transition? Better said, what are the transitions?

The company "grew" by the hire. So for an organization, growth is transition. It looks different than it did before. Much like adding on to a home, the company assimilates this new hire into its "home."

From the employee's point of view, the new job represents a morphing career. Additionally, the employee is transitioning into "ownership" in the sense that she "buys in" over time (this is genuine transition) to the mission and vision of the company. A new employee transitions well if she develops that kind of ownership over a period of time.

If we jump to the founder and to the end of his time with the firm he started, what does that transition look like? If we believe that it has three phases, let's start with the ending.

First, things aren't what they used to be. The founder must acknowledge that a death of sorts must occur. Many of us won't walk that plank voluntarily! We usually need a gun pointed at us to prompt us to jump into the sea. I know that because I've observed it many times. The impetus for the death is usually external to the founder—a health scare, literal death, or a mutiny. All of these external triggers may start the transition. But however the founder comes to terms with this "death," it must happen if transition is to occur.

Second, the neutral zone sets in. This can be a real no-man's-land where the founder flounders. He might think, "If I'm not "the guy," then who am I?" This can be a time of deep angst, or it can be a time of profound discovery.

I recently began working with a second-generation family business. Dad had to fight off a hostile takeover bid mounted by other family members. He recounted how, during the attempted "coup," he realized that the takeover could succeed and he actually could go do something else. What freedom came in that moment! Too many founders either die with their boots on or grumpily ride off into the sunset. Is there another way to walk graciously into the neutral zone?

Bridges would argue that the greatest change and growth can

occur in the neutral zone. Let the "desert" do its work in you! It can transform you if you let it.

Letting the neutral zone do the work that only it can do eventually will lead to the third stage, a new beginning—a resurrection of sorts. Consider many traditions in Asian cultures, which revere elders. A sage has an important role in an organization just as sages do within many Asian families. Along these lines, law firms often let older partners take on an "ex officio" role, which may be as simple as letting them keep their office for a while and so honor the know-how (and the know-who) of that partner. For the partner's sake, it may be a real season of meaning, purpose, and value.

Even if the aging partner doesn't remain "productive" in terms of billable hours, that doesn't mean the partner fails to add value to the firm. When the firm navigates these years wisely, it can allow that partner to bring to the company his or her most significant contributions.

This third stage of transition carries the notion that "we ain't done yet." There is something more. We haven't come to the end of the road. That mind-set is hopeful, not discouraging. There really is a Promised Land!

Yet how many founders fail to seize this opportunity? So many simply give in and end up as grumpy old men. Let me tell you, grumpy old men do exist. I've seen them and tried to work with them. None of us has as a life goal to become a grumpy old man! What will keep you and me from becoming one?

My mom died about ten years ago. Doctors diagnosed her with pancreatic cancer, and she died five weeks later. Her transition happened *fast*. After she died, I heard one comment repeatedly from those who knew her well: "She died well." That statement made a permanent mark on me. I want that to be said of me.

Will it be said of me only when I die physically? What about the many other "deaths" along the way? My mom "died early." That is to say, right after she learned of her diagnosis, she responded by saying, "Que será, será." At first, her words upset me; but later I realized that they reflected part of her dying well.

My dad, on the other hand, fought death. While I don't mean to be critical of him—in fact, I love, admire, and honor him maybe more today than I did sixteen years ago when he died—his downhill slide lasted fifteen months, and many times he verbalized his impatience, waiting for the doctors to discover what ailed him so they could "fix it" and he could get back to living. While I admire many aspects of this kind of fighting, when my time comes to die, whether physical death or one of the other kinds, I want to die well.

If it's your time to step away, step away well.

And if it's your time to step up, step up well.

A Transaction Isn't a Transition

"Exiters" don't know what good exiting looks like from the inside. While they may have observed others exit, they've never been there before themselves. And in my work, I can describe it only in the third person. Coco Chanel once said it well: "How many cares one loses when one decides not to be something but to be someone."[3] Bridges said in *The Way of Transition*:

> Your transition-generated journeys will always have destinations, and after the fact those destinations may turn out to be interesting enough to make others want to retrace your steps. But they cannot do so, for those steps were taken from where you actually were right then, and that is what gave them their vitality. (Your imitators could capitalize

on their own transition in the same way that you did, of course, but when they start to do so, they find a difficult ending ahead of them. That's when they decide to take the shortcut of imitation and skip the pain.) They try to turn wherever you ended up arriving into a place-to-aim-at, and then plan from Day One to arrive there. But the journey is the whole point. And besides it was your journey, not theirs . . . A "planned journey" is an oxymoron. The apple seed has no "plan" as it grows into a tree; there is no "plan" to the changes it goes through in response to the turning seasons. It is simply "apple-ing."[4]

Let me say it like this: just because a *transaction* happens doesn't mean the *transition* is complete!

There is transition and then there are transitions, plural. We're always transitioning in some way, shape, or form. Dad may want the kids to run the business eventually. But along the way, as Dad invites the kids into the conversation, he may say something like, "I really want them to decide." Conversation ensues. Maybe the kids agree on taking a track other than the one Dad would have preferred. Will Dad still "cut the check" in support of the kids' decision?

In your team's resolve to transition and keep transitioning well, remember that you are not alone. Most of the time, even as the elder still sits in the saddle, the next-gen leadership "can't wait" to take over. Resolve to resist the urge to dishonor the elder!

One client offered me a great perspective on transition: "We're going to get ourselves into a situation where shares will be inherited . . . and it will have to get sorted out . . . rather than being directed." Resolve to be proactive. Don't leave it to others to be reactive. As my partner says, "We either prepare or repair."

Remember that it's just as hard for the *founder* to transition to becoming a *follower* as it is for a *follower* to grow into the next-generation *leader* the company needs to move forward and thrive.

Resolve to not be an elder whom everyone tiptoes around. Remember Tiny Tim, the one-hit wonder who sang "Tiptoe Through the Tulips"? On our good days, we don't want people tiptoeing around us.

Face Your Fears

As we transition, we must resolve to face our fears. Consider just four statements made by a spouse as his wife began entering a transition toward retirement:

"She has to let go of where she's been."

"She gave up her office . . . gave up who she was."

"She has a fear of what she'll become, what she'll have to leave behind/let go of . . ."

"It feels a bit like she's going underground, becoming invisible, like entering the government's Witness Protection Program."

Resolve to begin this process with the understanding that we don't really *own* anything. We just get to use it for a while.

I once visited a long-time local farmer. He gave a single young man a life-estate interest in his farm. Ultimately it would go to the local soil conservation district, the university research center, or a land trust. I thought, "He's starting with the understanding that it won't be 'owned,' but stewarded—entrusted. Isn't that the way we should all view all of our resources?"

Too often with family businesses, the one who made the way is in the way, or certainly can be.

You've heard of women going to the hospital and giving birth without knowing they were pregnant? Well, I think there are a lot of family business owners "pregnant" with transition who don't know it. Transition will happen, one way or another. If you want a healthy "baby," it might be good to practice some quality "prenatal care."

I once spoke about transitions at a Soroptimist club in our town. After my presentation, a woman came up to me and told me how her husband, a scientist, had divorced his first wife. In the couple's division of assets, nine out of ten people in the man's circle of confidantes had encouraged him to leave a certain asset to his first wife. Only one person in that group advised him to hold onto it. He held onto it and now is finding it extremely difficult to let go and transition away from this business.

I'm reminded of the Old Testament story of King David's grandson, Rehoboam. When the young man came to power, he asked for counsel both from the old guys and the young guys. He disregarded the sage advice of his elders and instead followed the brash advice of his youthful peers, a choice that had disastrous consequences for the people of Israel. A civil war erupted, and the nation tore itself in two.[5]

Wise counsel matters when it comes to transition.

Watch for Different Paces

Just before going to a challenging meeting with a relatively new client, I got an idea while I was in the shower, where I seem to get a lot of my inspiration. I'd known the players for years, but only recently had they started getting serious about transition and only very recently had they formally and regularly engaged me as a facilitator. Here's the thought that came to me as I got cleaned up.

I like to mountain bike and consider myself a pretty good rider. Some of the guys I ride with race, and a racer I'm not. When I ride with the racers, they always beat me to the top of every climb. They often graciously wait for me at the top. But by the time I get there, they're ready to carry on while I'm ready for a break. I think, "What about me? When can I get a break?" And as we continue the ride, I head into my anger zone.

It's often like this in business transition. We all move at different paces. We have to wait on colleagues, and about the time they're ready to go, we're ready for a break, or vice versa. And does anger set in when another's pace doesn't match our own? You bet. Simply being aware of this difference in pace is useful. But even more useful is being gracious with colleagues.

As I went into that client meeting, I saw one member of the team forgetting to focus on being gracious. She exhibited, shall we say, some less-than-graceful behavior, but eventually she caught herself. After our meeting, the two of us had a brief one-on-one time and I mentioned that she needn't beat herself up about her lack of grace. We don't form new habits in a linear way; they usually form more like a spiral. We can hope the spiral goes up, not down, but we regularly "circle back" in our habits and behaviors and have to start over frequently. We need people around us who learn to be gracious with our spiraling. Yes, that can be tough slogging, but it's so worth it. James E. Hughes Jr. reminds us of the alternative.

In *Family: The Compact Among Generations*, Hughes says, "Unfortunately, the vast majority of succession plans and systems they develop don't work . . . The consensus on why they don't work is this: the rational solutions they offer can't overcome the irrational human behavior they must modify."[6]

Grace simply works better in overcoming irrational human

behavior than does logic. And it doesn't matter if we like the fact or not.

Listen to another nugget from Hughes: "To have the followers of a great family leader . . . continually feel as if they 'did it themselves' is the highest commendation any family leader can receive."[7] Rick McKinley, a Portland-area pastor, said essentially the same thing with different words. "Steward your moment," he said. "Then disappear."[8]

The Golden Word

As transition occurs from older to younger, I've found it particularly important that the elder hold up this sign: *YIELD!*

I watched it recently with a client. Dad gave input but then said, "I'm going to let you decide." It's harder to incorporate this in real time, however, than in a meeting! My subsequent e-mails and phone calls with the son-in-law made this apparent.

"It's like when Mark is here we do this," he told me, "but then when Mark isn't, we don't. I read the article you left [Bridges on "Wilderness"] . . . the more things change, the more they stay the same."

Throughout transition, it's important that we all learn to give ground from time to time. When the elder models this kind of "yielding," transition tends to go more smoothly. What would it look like if that Yield sign went up as a matter of habit? Would things stand a better chance of changing in a positive way?

What's Your Company Identity?

Another important aspect of transition is the company brand. What is the company's identity? With whom do customers identify?

I recently met with two owners of a family business with whom we've worked for several years. We discussed whether their customers would identify themselves as patrons of the owners or of the company.

If you want successful transition, you must strive to achieve the latter. Without effort, the customer will always, by default, identify with an individual and not with the company. Without intentionality, the customer simply will not identify with the brand of the company.

If you're part of the older generation in your company, I'm guessing you like the relationships you have with most, if not all, of your customers (although if we're honest, we can all probably think of one or two we might prefer to "graduate" to another company). Most of our small businesses are built upon relationships. Satisfied customers talk to each other, and our businesses grow primarily through networking and referral.

But to grow beyond mom-and-pop, where everybody knows everybody within the company and in the customer base, *something* has to change. As this change occurs, you not only enhance the customer experience with the company, but you build enterprise value in your business. Any future potential buyer/owner knows (or should know) that if all the relationships depend on you, when you're taken out of the picture, the value of the business plummets.

Consider a few suggestions that can assist the older generation in helping the next generation to retain customers and transfer their loyalty to the company.

- Find ways to endorse the next generation's competencies. Do this when communicating directly with your key customers.

- Take an extended time away. When customers call or come in, they will interact with others in the company.
- When both generations meet with a key customer, intentionally make room for the next generation's input. Try asking, "Johnny, what do you think would be the wise thing for our customer to do here?" (Even if you lose business by making what might seem to be a risky move here, the confidence you show in the next generation in front of a key customer will go a long way in building the next generation's confidence.)
- Use "we" statements as opposed to "I" statements in front of customers.
  - "Our policy is..."
  - "We at Company X place a high priority on contacting our key customers x times per year. Sometimes you'll hear from me, but if it's okay, Johnny may invite you to lunch in June..."
- Try scheduling a meeting with a key customer. At the start of the meeting, let the customer know you're going to have to leave the meeting at a certain time, before the meeting is scheduled to end. Ask if it would be okay if Johnny finished the meeting. Even if you've covered all the items on the agenda, if the customer can spend the last half hour with Johnny, the relationship will grow—without you.

Relationships are built upon trust, and trust takes time to develop. You can help the process or you can hinder it. Do the former and not the latter!

While you will probably never be completely free from the

way customers identify you with the company, think about what it would feel like to end up with customers expressing loyalty to the company and not just to one specific individual. What would it feel like for you? For your next-gen owners? For the customer experience?

While it is self-evident that this should happen, it does not happen naturally. A tension exists between holding on and letting go, for both customers and owners. Do all you can to help all parties let go. If you succeed, you will move the company away from mom-and-pop to a real company, its own entity, a business benefitting both next-gen owners and customers.

Embrace the Mystery

While we can make choices and play a huge role in our own transition and in the transitions we are part of, an element of mystery also exists in this thing called transition. Part of transition happens to you—it's done in you. In a sense, at times it even happens without you or despite you.

Look at a caterpillar. Do you know how it becomes a butterfly? Something very obscure and unfathomable takes place in this transition from caterpillar, through cocoon, to butterfly. I suppose William Bridges would say the caterpillar ends, the cocoon is the neutral zone, and the butterfly is the new beginning. And they occur in that definite order.

Looking at this kind of transition, much like observing the birth of a child, feels a bit intrusive, as though we're walking on holy ground. When we watch the "transition" of a newborn infant or watch a butterfly emerge from its cocoon, it's as though we are witnessing the mysteries of the universe unlocked before us. I certainly can't do this for myself or for others! We play cops and robbers, cowboys and Indians, frogs and princesses, but this is *true* change. All else is pretend.

And yet this true change, this transition, comes from somewhere. This kind of change is genuine metamorphosis—a radical transformation. It's beautiful to watch, but spectacular to be a part of.

- part four -

COMMIT

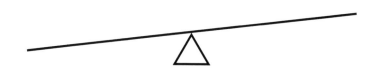

A CALL TO ALL TEAM MEMBERS
TO MOVE BEYOND TALK TO ACTION

THIRTEEN

personal trainer

Have you ever tried hiring a personal trainer? Whether or not you have, ask yourself why you might hire one. Let me guess a few of your answers.

- "I've tried New Year's resolutions before. They last at most a month."
- "I've tried working out with a buddy. That worked for a while. But then..."
- "The trainer provides accountability."
- "Since I pay for a personal trainer, I want to get my money's worth."
- "Paying the fee is a bit of skin in the game. It makes it more likely that I'll get my behind out of bed and show up at the gym and do my workout."
- "The trainer has been through this before. I trust she knows what she's doing."

How'd I do?

When people ask me to describe what we do in Family Business Counsel, I often describe our work in terms of a personal trainer. For reasons similar to those listed above, I know it's far more likely you will balance the family business teeter totter with the help of a "personal trainer."

But It's Hard!

I know it's hard for leaders to ask for help. Most of the time, it takes a crisis, much like what it takes for many people to finally go to counseling.

"I don't need to see a shrink," they will say. "Shrinks are for people with real problems."

Is that how you view it? I certainly used to, until I really had no choice. When my dad died, I felt as though I was carrying the load for my whole family—not only for my nuclear family, but for my brother and sister as well. I needed help sorting through things. But I didn't reach out to get that help until I felt I had reached the end of my rope. And the counseling helped! I now see it as a courageous move when people who need help seek out a counselor.

But who counsels business owners? I don't mean a consultant, but a counselor, a confidant, someone who can act as a sounding board for the business owner. While a CPA or an attorney could play the role, most don't feel comfortable talking about the "touchy/feely stuff." And how do they get paid? By the hour, on the clock. But we'll never get to the issues we absolutely have to address if the client is worried about the meter running.

Well then, how about financial professionals? How might they serve as counselors? While I know that some practice "life planning," in my experience, most financial advisors tend to say, "I'm not trained in psychology, so I can't go there."

Conversely, most psychologists aren't trained in business matters. Neither are clergy.

So where does that leave the business owner who admits he or she needs help but has nowhere to turn? That's the gap we've tried to step into. And I'm an evangelist when it comes to this approach! Every business, family, team, and organization needs facilitation. We all need facilitators in one area or another. That's why I like what the poet Rumi said: "Close both eyes to see with the other eye." For family businesses, we're often that other eye.

Before the Crisis Hits

I recently attended a gathering of advisors who work with family enterprises. An interviewer asked the CEO of a local family business how advisors could render better assistance to family firms like his. He didn't hesitate. "Get to them through some sort of forum before crisis hits," he said.

We've tried to do this by facilitating forums where family members and key employees of family businesses come together. We typically divide them into the "older" group and the "younger" group and then pose questions to each group for discussion:

- What do you wish the "other guys" knew about you?
- What bothers you about the "other guys"?

Finally, we bring both groups together and watch what happens. It's always lively! The participants always gain several important takeaways:

- We aren't the only ones facing these issues.
- Maybe we can talk about this stuff.
- Maybe we need some help facilitating these challenging conversations.

While it's better to have the necessary conversations before a crisis hits, sometimes you have no choice but to have them after an explosion. A few key questions can help set the stage for changing the tone of the conversation, particularly if you have already moved into crisis mode.

Prior to an initial meeting with two business owners who had fallen into crisis mode, I asked both clients to think about a couple of things:

- How did we get here?
- What are the core issues?

I wanted to use these two questions to get our new clients to agree on a few ground rules for moving forward. For us to make progress, they had to find something they could agree on. They needed something solid to build on, a belief that they could, one day, create a new, healthy culture of communication. It really can happen, even after a crisis hits.

Sometimes, in order to go from crisis to a healthier culture, one specific ground rule must be imposed temporarily. The parties in conflict can communicate with each other only in the presence of the facilitator. In some cases, so much relational damage has been done that the crisis stage has a "nothing-good-comes-from-that" atmosphere. It may take a while, but with hard work and a rebuilding of trust, the parties can get to the point where at least they can say, "Good morning," and not read anything disparaging into the greeting. Over time, they can see that not every interaction has to lead to an explosion. Bit by bit, they can move out of crisis mode and into "recovery," which eventually can lead to a healthier culture.

But remember, most change like this happens slowly. Be patient.

Not long ago, I met with a father and two sons, all of them engaged with a family business in at least its third generation, if not its fourth. The family had weathered some storms and was in the midst of another when they asked to meet with me. Because of the conflict, one brother had already left, twice.

Since it was a fairly athletic family, I thought we could draw on a sports analogy. I asked if they remembered playing pickup basketball games, where a bunch of guys get together to play an informal game. When you play these pickup games, you don't have referees. As a result, you try to follow an honor system and call your own fouls.

I asked these guys how that usually worked out. Often, they said, not so well. I agreed. I remember a lot of arguments. Sometimes the one who brought the game ball took his ball and went home. Other times shouting matches erupted. Sometimes the game just ended. Sometimes it ended in a fight.

Not so unlike family businesses, is it? Games usually go better with referees.

"I'm the referee," I told them.

We all laughed. They got the message, loud and clear.

Change the Conversation, Change the Business

Not long ago I had a phone conversation with a friend who owns a small business. He asked me to clarify the difference between viewing his business as a tool for generating income (paycheck) and viewing it as an asset. I explained that a paycheck is something I collect on a regular basis; it's mine. An asset, on the other hand, is something I steward or take care of. It's bigger than just me.

As we spoke, I sensed the lightbulb go on. "I'd never looked at that way," he said. And thus began a process of discovery for my friend. He wanted to explore how he could pass on to someone else, potentially a next-gen owner, something that had value.

What else can happen when a business owner allows an "outsider" to facilitate?

One client said to me, "Mark, there are things that wouldn't get said without you in the room." I noted three implications of his statement:

1. It's good to "get stuff on the table." The power of dark secrets gets broken when light shines in a dark place.
2. We don't always want to hear what needs to be spoken. And when we hear it, we need two things: time to process what we've heard, and a setting in which to process the relational part of the insight.
3. You can construct a "safe house" in which these helpful conversations can take place.

Why do I choose to do what I do? I believe that my best comes out when conversations get stuck. People call each other ugly names and threaten to walk out of meetings. Somehow, the conversation keeps going and the individuals keep coming to the meetings. I do this work because I believe that countless conversations should be happening that are not happening—and that needs to change. Whether it's a family, an organization, a business, or some other team, if we are to envision a hopeful, thriving future and then see that future unfold, these conversations must take place. And for that to happen, the culture of communication within these teams needs to morph.

Rarely have I seen these conversations take place on their own. Someone outside must come inside. Space must be cracked open. When this occurs, people find the room that enables them to speak and hear differently, and so the conversation changes. If we can change the conversation, we can change the ethos of the team and thereby help the team succeed.

When any family, organization or other team commits to this path, they often discover it includes at least three positive outcomes:

- A growing level of honesty
- A belief that moving forward can bring real hope
- An attempt to seek win/win outcomes

Have you heard of DKDK? *We don't know what we don't know.* This statement is true for all of us. None of us knows what we don't know. At Family Business Counsel, we sometimes think of ourselves as librarians. Every client story is a reference volume we can pull off the shelf to help every other client. What we learned in that situation over there, we can use to help you in your situation over here.

As we help facilitate these crucial conversations, we've noticed something taking place often. Invariably, if the current owners are in their midfifties or older, we hear them say, "We should have started these conversations five or ten years ago."

The truth is, once you crack open the door, many benefits of facilitation open up. And this can happen in families as well as in businesses.

One Christmas, everyone in our family got to pick a day when every person in our clan would do whatever the "person of the day" chose. I wanted to spend my day watching Eddie Murphy movies, so we took in flicks such as *Beverly Hills Cop*, *Coming to America*, *Trading Places*, and *The Nutty Professor*. By the end of the day, I'd had my fill of Eddie Murphy. I won't tell you how my family interpreted the day. Let's just say they were good sports and "let Dad have his day."

My wife, on the other hand, teed up a day that forever changed our family. She wanted each of us to take the Myers-Briggs personality inventory, the venerable personal assessment tool. We engaged a facilitator, each of us did the assessment individually, and then we spent time as a family talking through our profiles with the help of this facilitator. What an incredible day!

We discovered, for example, that words as basic as *honesty* can mean different things to different people. To my son, honesty means truthfully answering Mom's questions. To my wife, honesty means full disclosure. So, hypothetically, when Lyn asks Drew what he did last night, and Drew says he hung out with friends—and later Lyn finds out he also snuck into a gym with his friends to play basketball, without permission, and left some lights on—she says, "He lied. He wasn't honest. Therefore, I can't trust him."

I think you can begin to see the value of the time we spent as a family on Myers-Briggs! The space the facilitator opened up felt incredibly enlightening to all of us.

About a year later, we engaged a facilitator to do the same thing with our company. The facilitator made an interesting observation. She described our company as "introverted," which has implications for how we tell our story and how we market ourselves. Because we are an introverted company, *we* know what we do . . . but no one else does. That's not a great marketing strategy!

As a result of this insight, we engaged a marketing firm for twelve months and, through its facilitation, found a better way to tell our story. We renamed the company. Designed a new logo. Launched a new website. Clarified our vision.

Why did all of this happen? It happened because we allowed "outsiders" to facilitate some crucial work in our company. These days, we actively encourage all our family business clients to consider this kind of facilitation.

How Does It Work?

A potential client once asked me, "So Mark, are you going to show us the blueprint for this?" I told him that if he was going to engage our services, he was going to have to strike *blueprint* from his vocabulary.

The work of facilitation is more like going on a walkabout than a day hike. For a day hike, you hire a guide who gives you a map, pointing out where you'll take pictures, where you'll eat lunch, and how far you'll hike, along with what time you can expect to be back at your car. The aboriginal guide who takes you on your walkabout says, "I know we'll eat, but I can't tell you when or where. I know we'll sleep under the stars, but I'm not sure where. We'll be back, but I don't know when. You'll experience things you've never experienced. Trust me! I've been on this walk many times."

It takes courage to go on a walkabout rather than a day hike—but the benefits of the former can far outweigh those of the latter. I think that's why one consultant calls what we do "Braveheart Consulting." He understands that it takes courage to change.

Using "The Orange"

I once heard professional mediator Raphael Lapin share a story called "The Orange" that has helped many groups to move forward. We often use it in our own work. Lapin describes how Johnny and Susie, brother and sister, are fighting over an orange. They both desperately want the orange.

Now, Dad could swoop in with the Solomon approach and offer to cut the orange in two. That way, at least, both Johnny and Susie would get something, although only 50 percent of what they want. Instead, Dad takes Johnny aside and asks why he's so interested in the orange. Johnny replies that he has been outside running around all day and that a big, juicy orange would go a long way toward quenching his thirst. Dad then goes to Susie and asks about her interest in the orange. Susie replies that Mom has shared a cake recipe with her and that the frosting calls for the zest of the orange peel.

Dad quickly realizes that both Johnny and Susie can get 100 percent of what *really* interests them, not just what they think they want. Johnny can get the juice; Susie can get the peel. This happens only because he digs below their wants to discover their true individual interests.[1] Peeling back the layers can get to core issues. And it can bring about some honest sharing.

I often ask another question to peel back another layer in the midst of conflict: "What do you think should happen here?" Initially, one party will often describe his side and his preferred outcome. A facilitator can clearly see that this isn't "fair." At that point, the facilitator can state, "So what you're telling me is you want more than your fair share. Am I hearing you correctly?" This statement holds a mirror in front of the person so he can see himself clearly, but without the "enemy" trapping him. This allows for honest confession that usually prompts a change in posture and opens a new way forward.

One attorney describes our work as being "The Business Whisperer." I like that.

I recently stumbled on another tool that can open the door to using "The Orange." Two owners of a professional services firm had reached a seemingly insurmountable obstacle in their path to an amenable future, which included eventual exits for both of them. They each told me privately that the other's proposal was unacceptable, and so I felt anxious about our upcoming meeting.

When we got together, with more than a little fear and

trepidation, I drew a circle on the back of our agenda. "Assume this represents all there is," I said. "Now, what do you want, Mr. Jones? And what do you want, Mr. Smith? If we add up those two and the sum is more than the circle, something's got to give." I call this "the math of circles and addition." In their case, the impasse I had assumed was there didn't really exist. About two minutes after I drew the circle, they were able to reach a mutually agreeable solution.

The simple act of drawing a circle got us all to look at things a little differently. If it hadn't, perhaps the math of circles and addition would have led us to "The Orange."

Finding a Facilitator

When a facilitator functions at a high level, the team gets not only a listening ear, but also a seeing eye. Let me give a word of caution here, however. I've often watched "the old guy" speak for the younger generation—usually incorrectly. It's easy for a facilitator to think, "They shouldn't do that." But thinking a thought differs from acting on that thought.

The fact is, as a facilitator I can assume way too much and end up speaking for someone else. It is of utmost importance to let people describe their own experience and their own feelings. Don't do it for them! Even if my assumptions turned out to be right, allowing individuals to articulate their own position and their own feelings is important. As a facilitator, I dare not rob them of the growth and life that comes from being able to tell their own story in their own words.

I've had to hone my fishing skills as I've worked with family businesses. A good fisherman knows when to let a fish run and when to reel it in. A good facilitator knows how to do the same with client conversations. Sometimes they need to run and sometimes they need to be reeled in.

Sometimes in those conversations we need to face the music. There is bad news "out there." But the bad news isn't the end of the story. Most of us will never face what Viktor Frankl had to face in a Nazi concentration camp. In his seminal work *Man's Search for Meaning*, Frankl stated, "Everything can be taken from a man but one thing: the last of the human freedoms—to choose one's attitude in any given set of circumstances, to choose one's own way."[2] I hope you will cling to that "one thing" that remains whenever you face bad news. May you choose to find hope and a way forward—perhaps with a facilitator—to persevere and press on.

What about the Cost?

I recently spoke on a panel with a retired family business owner who had worked through his transition plan for his family's business. It intrigued me to hear him describe why and how they decided to hire a facilitator. He described his efforts on his own to convene and facilitate crucial conversations with the family business. "I got to the point where I realized I needed to be a participant in these conversations," he said. "I couldn't be a facilitator."

He said his family had budgeted $180,000 over two years to hire their family business "personal trainer." Was it worth it? "It was the best money we ever spent," he declared.

My wife attended that forum, and during the Q&A, she raised her hand and asked to speak (which frankly made me nervous). She said that when she first heard me describe my fees—not as high as what the retiree on our panel paid, by the way—she insisted she would never pay that kind of money. But when I talked about farmers not blinking to spend a quarter million dollars or more on a piece of equipment or regularly hiring people for $30,000 or more per year, it began to make sense to her.

You can think about the cost from the opposite direction too. That is, how much will it cost you in the long run to *not* get the help you need? For a moment, let me pick on dentists. Dentists know that many patients wait too long to get their toothaches taken care of, which results in more pain, excruciating root canals, and far more expense. What does it cost to put off getting the required treatment? A lot! Both dentists and their patients get that. But how often do dentists fail to follow their own recommendations when it comes to creating the office culture they want for themselves, their staff, and their patients? What does it cost them to put off getting the help they need to create their desired office culture? It might be huge!

Facilation isn't cheap, and you get what you pay for. In choosing a facilitator, it's all about the fit. From my point of view, facilitation will only work if your whole team buys in to the facilitator and the process he or she lays out. Lack of buy-in will quickly derail everything.

How Long Does It Take?

Sometimes people ask me, "How do we know when we're done?" Facilitation is like using training wheels when you're learning to ride a bike. You generally know when you no longer need the training wheels. You stop using them when you know you can ride on your own.

As a facilitator, I serve as the training wheels for a family business. I shouldn't do for you what you can do for yourself. But I also know it takes time to build those muscles, to learn to get ahead of crucial conversations heading your way. A good facilitator is a guide more than an expert who tells you everything to do. This is *your* work. I can give you helpful tools, but they'll do you no good if they stay in the tool shed. You must implement the implements.

So when people ask how long the facilitation process takes, I often reply, without trying to be a smart aleck, "Longer than you think." We always discover new issues during the process. People change. It's one of the reasons we won't do hourly billing. As I've said, if the client worries about the meter running, we'll never get to the issues we truly need to address.

Time to Walk the Path?

I know these aren't easy areas for family businesses to wade into.

"What will others think? That we're screwed up?"

"Does nobody else deal with this?"

"This isn't rocket science. Surely we can handle this on our own."

"They (the kids) will just have to deal with it."

"We don't talk about family with 'outsiders.'"

I have just one question for you: How's that working out for you?

Not long ago, I signed up to do something that made me cringe. I arranged to have a booth in the exhibition center at an industry association conference. While I saw a few smiling faces, mostly I just sat there for fear that people would see me as a beggar. I tended to think of it like this: "Here I am, with my cardboard sign, asking for handouts."

When one friendly face came by, we started talking about how much I detested having a booth. All of a sudden, he told me of an idea he had for our company slogan:

"Is your family as f*%#ed up as ours? Go see Mark!"

I have to find a way to put that on my business card!

Will it take a crisis to get you to ask for help? It's okay to ask for help. It really is. And, what's the alternative? If you don't ask for help, and your son or daughter feels afraid to tell you that he or she doesn't want to join the family business, what happens? Either they suck it up and do something they're not cut out to do, or, they "elope"—they run off and don't tell you. Pick which one you want.

I'm guessing it's neither.

Now let me paint a different picture for you.

Suppose you swallow your pride and face your fears. I've had to do both innumerable times in my relationship with my business partner, "the founder."

So you decide it's okay to ask for help.

You let an outsider in.

You start to talk about "what we can't talk about."

When difficult issues arise, you know you have a regular time and place to talk about them in a safe environment.

You create a culture of communication in your family business.

You find out you aren't alone, that other family businesses deal with similar issues.

You break the power of the secret.

Sure, you have a few setbacks along the way. You have to let go of preferred, predetermined outcomes.

You begin to have confidence that even if things don't always go according to plan, they can continue to move forward.

You become convinced that if conversation continues, you'll make progress.

You begin to believe that the business can not only survive without you, but thrive.

You begin to see a sort of emeritus role emerge for you. Once you communicate that you don't want to be in the way, the younger generation begins to see you as a sage; they ask for your opinion and seek your counsel.

You see that you can be away for increasingly longer periods of time . . . and they survive without you.

You begin to believe that the company can go to new heights once you are gone.

So let me ask a question: What would a scenario like that be worth to you, to your family, and to your business?

Are you ready to commit to walk this path?

FOURTEEN

▼

integrity

What comes to mind when you ponder *integrity*? Do you think of a reliable person, someone whose stellar character matches his or her commitment to speaking truth?

The word *integrity* has its roots in the word *integer*. An integer is a whole number. Part of what it means to have integrity, therefore, is to be whole.

Are you a whole person? We all want to be whole, both inside and out. Some say integrity is who you are when no one is looking. While our lives have different parts, integrity seeks to integrate these parts. It helps us to avoid becoming so compartmentalized that we lose the whole.

We're All Broken

Let's face it, we're all broken, in some ways broken to pieces. And yet, there remains a possibility of Humpty Dumpty being put back together again. If we're really to be made whole, however, we have to start by recognizing our brokenness.

When we get broken, most of us find a way to survive. But in our attempts to survive, we remain stuck in that old place. Sometimes it's only decades later that we finally come to that awareness. It's something like PTSD, post-traumatic stress disorder. While I don't want to minimize what a traumatized soldier experiences in a war zone, most of us adapt and survive our own "wars," and some sort of disorder usually ensues.

Pam's mom died when Pam was just nine years old. Pam got the news during a year-end school picnic. Three days later, she found herself on a plane to Grandma's house for the summer because Dad was on the road all the time as a traveling salesman. While she enjoyed the summer with Grandma, the visit ended too quickly and she returned to school, trying to find a way forward with the rest of her life.

Decades later, Pam works as the controller for her husband's third-generation family business. She regularly finds herself getting easily agitated by what she considers "financial improprieties." When people began to wonder about her emotional outbursts in meetings, Pam started to unpack some of where she's been "stuck" these past four decades. Little by little, she's coming to terms with what happened way back when. These days, new patterns of engagement are starting to emerge.

This progress isn't linear. Often it's three steps forward, two steps back. Pam commented recently that she's begun to realize how she'd become such an angry person. She's now grateful that this "beast" is being tamed. The ripple effects of that taming are impacting every area of her life.

Pam is beginning to feel whole again.

Match Words with Actions

People with integrity strive to make their actions match their words. But for this chapter, I'd like to turn that around for a moment. Sometimes we need to *say* what we *do*.

Others often draw their own conclusions about the meaning of what they see us doing. If we don't tell them what our actions mean, we could end up on very different pages. This idea has particular importance for teams.

Suppose that part of a team makes a decision but doesn't communicate that decision to the rest of the team. The decision makers nevertheless carry out that decision, resulting in confusion and even conflict. Who wants that?

If you make a new hire for an established position, for example, but without any announcement you privately change the duties and responsibilities of the position, confusion and conflict almost certainly will result. I can hear it now from the employee's predecessor: "Hey! That is *my* area! She's sticking her nose into my business!"

More than a year into an engagement with a client, we realized that the last time someone like me had visited their office, a major family explosion had occurred, prompting several people to leave or lawyer up. All hell broke loose. We realized that we had better communicate that I had not come to create yet another explosion! We needed to communicate that things were good with the family and that people could relax about their jobs.

This is what I mean about the need to match our words with our actions. Announce what you are doing, which is simply another version of integrity. Get out in front of crucial conversations.

Do What You Say

Now, let's carry integrity to another element of team. If we talk about the culture we want but don't act on it, our behavior also reflects a lack of integrity. Do what you say you're going to do. If you don't, you will strongly demotivate your team.

Say what you mean and mean what you say. Actions do speak louder than words.

I interviewed a key employee at a family business, a young man who served in management but wasn't a member of the owner family. He shared his frustration that sometimes family employees were not held accountable for their actions, and therefore team morale suffered.

Over time, however, the team took action to raise its standards, and the young man saw a new seriousness in the way family member employees handled their responsibilities. His buy-in increased enormously as he saw not just words and good intentions but real action congruent with those words and intentions.

An Integrated, Purposeful Life

You may have seen the diagram below. It shows an integrated life, a life of purpose. I have a sign in my office that says, "The purpose of life is a life of purpose." That is what it means to live a whole life.

I give clients an exercise that we call "bull's-eye." It gets at these things through five Cs.

Calling: What is my purpose?
Competencies: What do others say I'm good at?
Character: How is my character being formed?
Community: Am I functioning within the context of community?

Courage: Do I have the courage to implement what I've just discovered about myself?

People who operate in their bull's-eye know who they are. They've wrestled the issue of identity to the ground. They've had to ask themselves if they're trying to be the person they're "supposed" to be or the person they're made to be. When you don't know who you are, you're wishy-washy. When you do know who you are, integrity comes more easily (although it's never easy).

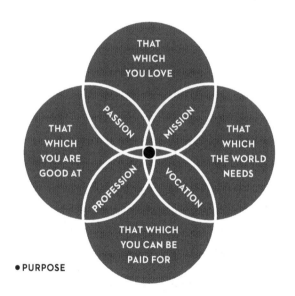

The Ten Commandments of Functional Teams

We've developed something at Family Business Counsel that, if implemented, can go a long way toward validating your integrity with your team. We call this the "Ten Commandments of Functional Teams" (and yes, I realize we have more than ten items here):

- There is a difference between what we *intend* and how our actions *impact* others.
- Ask yourself, "How badly do I want this? Does it fit me? What do others think?"
- Consider the currency of buy-in and ownership. Is it only money, or does it include responsibility and meaningful work?
- Identify the *seers* (probably leaders) in your organization.
- Don't base *assessments* on *assumptions*.
- Work on *diplomacy*. What's in your head often isn't what you communicate to others.
- Clarify the difference between *leadership* and *management*.
- Build a culture of trust. Trust is hard to build and easy to lose.
- Be clear in your communication and identify what hat you are wearing when you communicate. Are you speaking to the person as a peer or are you operating as a superior, i.e. providing hierarchical accountability?
- Once a management/leadership role is assigned, the owners must endorse the role assignments.
- As you give feedback, ask yourself, "What would it take for this person to feel good about this constructive criticism?"
- Begin developing Cultural Covenants with smaller teams. "These are five or six things we all agree to." Once agreed upon, post them at each person's workstation. Agree that each team member can enforce the covenant. Hold each other accountable. The team wants it and will raise the bar.

- Push conversations back in the direction they came from. Don't settle for hearsay. "Is that what really happened? Why don't you go clarify what she meant by that?"

When a team can reach agreement on things like the above, they can develop a common language. When we write them down and put them somewhere public, we focus on them. And what we focus on, we move toward. As we move toward them, integrity (integration between words and actions) follows.

Integrated Character

In his outstanding book titled *Integrity*, Dr. Henry Cloud says,

> Character is the ability to meet the demands of reality.... The key here for our look at character is twofold: First, integrated character does not avoid negatives, but does the opposite—actively seeks them out to resolve them. Second, integrated character does not see facing negatives only as something painful, but as an opportunity to make things better and get to a good place.[1]

Cloud lists six key aspects of integrated character:

1. The ability to connect authentically
2. The ability to be oriented toward truth
3. The ability to work in a way that gets results and finishes well
4. The ability to embrace, engage, and deal with the negative
5. The ability to be oriented toward growth [personal growth, the growth of the team, etc.]
6. The ability to be transcendent[2]

Would you agree that someone who lives out these aspects of character is a "whole" person? *Whole*, as we have seen, is another way to describe someone living an integrated life, a life of integrity.

Integrated Heart, Desire, and Passion

Leaders who want to live out their integrity work hard to embody that integrity with their team. Cloud says,

> If you gain people's trust, their heart, then you also have their desire and passion. Heart, desire, and passion all go together. . . . That is why some leaders only get compliance, but can't capture their people's best efforts. It is why some parents get obedience in the short term, but not autonomous kids who desire to be the best for them that they can be. These leaders and parents just impose their will on the other people.[3]

At some point, you don't want kids to mimic the elders' behavior, but to boldly go where no man has gone before. You want them to go where they believe they need to go, or even better, where they believe they're called to go. It's hard to get much better than that.

Wanting Another's Best

People of integrity want the best for those in vital relationship to them. If I want the best for me, shouldn't I want the best for others? A bit of Golden Rule here. If I want others to think and believe the best about me, shouldn't I do the same for them? This kind of consistency communicates integrity. And when that kind of integrity is part of a culture, trust is built. Trust communicates that we aren't going to be afraid to face tough issues together. When I show that I trust you, I have your back and know you have mine. Together we can find synergy to achieve things we couldn't otherwise. A culture that is characterized by these traits is full of people looking out for the best interest of the other. And when I know this is true, I give you my best, even when my supervisor isn't around. Isn't that one definition of integrity? It's who you are when no one's looking.

I believe there's integrity in letting go. As I've said, I've watched elders start to let go and then take it back. It becomes something like a bait and switch. I want something, so in order to get it, I lead you to believe you're going to get something you want . . . and then I take it back. That's not good either for integrity or for the welfare of the business.

Deep Humility and Strong Will

In his book *Good to Great*, Jim Collins developed a concept he called "Level 5 Leadership." As I ponder how Collins described this type of leader, a different slant on integrity emerges. Think of the integrated whole and how good leaders balance the tension between two key traits. Collins said a Level 5 Leader is characterized by both *extreme personal humility* and *intense professional will*.[4] Let's flesh this out a bit.

Is it possible to be both humble and strong-willed at the same time? To be a humble leader who relishes the idea of others around him flourishing, who does all he can to make this happen, who shares and even deflects earned credit, who is known for "we" statements more than "I" statements? And who at the same time possesses a dogged determination, characterized by ever-clarifying vision and a ruthless perseverance, despite the challenges and even threats faced regularly by those who desire to lead well?

Who wouldn't want to follow that kind of leader?

FIFTEEN

governance: the rules around here

A family business in the Midwest is trying to get to the third generation. Mom and Dad started the business from scratch, and a brother and sister expanded the business to a total of fourteen retail outlets. Brother and Sister are looking toward retirement, and now four cousins are getting ready to take over.

One of the cousins went to his uncle to complain about how he's being mistreated by his three cousins. He said he's getting picked on. The uncle told his kids, who took the information back into a management meeting—resulting in a big blowup.

"Why did you go talk to your uncle instead of talking to us?" they demanded.

How could this situation have been avoided? I can think of one way in a single word: governance. Having ground rules in place can save you all kinds of trouble.

What Are Our Rules of Engagement?

Toward the beginning of *Family Business Key Issues*, authors Denise Kenyon-Rouvinez and John Ward make an important point: "Since it is a living document, the protocol/constitution can be revised, expanded, or reduced."[1] We tell clients that *documents get dusty*. They need to be dynamic, not just some paper stored in a forgotten notebook somewhere.

Certainly not all families have a family charter or a written protocol or constitution. But written or not, intentional or not, all family businesses have rules of engagement. Even if the only rule is there are no rules, you have rules. Without some form of governance, every issue faced can become a "one-off"—and one-offs can wear you out. If policy or governance is in place, then when violations happen (and they will), the policy or the charter is the bad guy, not the person. This is huge!

Kenyon-Rouvinez and Ward make a distinction between a formal family governance policy and what they call a *family council*. The family council can be made up of a mix of shareholders/nonshareholders, employees, and family members not working in the business. Both blood and in-laws can be included. The authors make a strong point about the family council by stating that one role of family council is to anticipate conflict.[2] You have heard of BS meters? Well, who has the conflict meter in your family? The authors contend:

> When the family has established its basic direction . . . Parents are reluctant to suffer the anger and resentment of their children regarding perceived injustices. In the case of

inheritance, they are more likely to take the easy path, sometimes creating chaos and conflict in the next generation. Parents are in a much better position than are their children to determine the right ownership group for the company. They could at least create buy-sell agreements, valuation policies, and other ownership agreements so that their children do not have to wrestle with these issues. But because they do not want to rock the boat, have inadequate professional advice, or are poor planners, most parents miss their chance to put into place structures and agreements that will help their children deal with messy ownership issues later.[3]

When it comes to governance, as with a lot of things, we can be proactive or reactive. Part of governance is the way we make decisions. In your governance, be bold. Take the reins. Studies have shown that we have only so much willpower. Instead of having to make a new decision every time a new problem appears, policy and procedure can save some of that willpower for the unforeseen inevitabilities that come to all family businesses.

Who Can Own Stock?

Who can own stock in your company? You'd better make this part of governance or it will spark hot debate.

We have a relatively new client. A couple started a business and now has three kids and a son-in-law working in it. Mom and Dad once heard something a family business advisor stated at a conference: "Only blood can own stock." That statement is now hardwired into their family business. I would say it is part of their governance.

I've heard the son-in-law say, "I bust my ass to make this company go. I get it, but I don't want to be part of the conversation about stock transfers." He then painted a picture of his situation: "There's a table . . . I don't get to sit at the table, but my kids do." Is that how you want to handle stock ownership in your family business?

Interestingly, a tipping point came for this client during a team meeting when Dad said, "Your mom and I are going to leave the stock in the company to the three families." This statement became a game changer. We pushed pause and parked there for a while. What everyone had heard (remember intent vs. impact) from Dad and Mom was, "We're leaving the stock to the *kids*." But there's a difference between *kids* and *families*. One word changes the game.

By the way, these tipping points/points of inflection occur in every family business. They are almost always unpredictable, but when they occur, the game changes.

Make sure you discuss who can own stock! This issue often comes up when you hire an attorney to draft a shareholder agreement. How you get in and how you get out are two key discussion topics as you develop your shareholder agreement. Who can own stock is a top-of-the-list question you must address.

Let me encourage you to take your time before you sign a shareholder agreement. Attorneys can give you a boilerplate document, but do you know what you signed? We just helped a client navigate three distinct drafts supplied by an attorney. We probably had five meetings with the shareholders, working through the issues involved in a well-thought-out shareholder agreement. Start to finish, it probably took seven months. When we had the shareholders sign, the attorney said, "I'd much rather have this kind of process for a client than the, 'Here, sign this!' approach." We actually read the document out loud in one meeting. And the client kept notes from all of the meetings so that in five years when someone rereads the shareholder agreement, they can have a way to recall why they made certain decisions on various provisions of the agreement.

If you don't go through this rigorous process, you run the risk I described earlier of hardwiring dysfunction for generations.

I'll conclude this section with another quote from Kenyon-Rouvinez and Ward on ownership of family businesses: "In countries where there are no or low estate taxes, parents are tempted to keep the ownership during their lifetimes. This is generally a mistake for both business and family reasons. It is usually much better for the business for the new business leader or leaders to have ownership control within a few years of assuming the responsibility of running the company. The senior generation has every right and incentive to test the new business leaders."[4]

Test driving ownership has its share of pros and cons. A pro is seeing how some next-gen family members conduct themselves once they own even one share of the company's stock. This will give you a good indicator of next-gen readiness to sit in "the big seats."

What Family Members Can Work Here?

Before we address the topic of adult children, let's talk about young children. I suggest you bring them with you to work. Involve them in company events. After all, we are discussing *family* business. Don't leave your family, in this case your young children, out of the business!

Nevertheless, there is a place to build a wall of separation. Don't tie up all of the family's net worth in the business, for example, and don't let the family farm become the governing body for all family decisions. The latter is a surefire way to alienate two classes of people: kids and in-laws. If the family farm is king, your kingdom will not long have subjects.

Expose your young children to the business, including its customers and employees. Let them do some odd jobs. Give them a chance to see if they might be interested in the family business. When they become adults, however, I concur with many experts "out there." While the following list is not meant to be exhaustive, it does highlight several areas of critical importance if you're thinking about employing adult children.

- Adult children have to work elsewhere for a minimum of three to five years.
- During that work experience, they must receive multiple promotions.
- If and when they return to the family business, they will be hired to do a job for which they are qualified, like any other applicant. (Be careful about creating a special position for one of your children.)
- Be careful about rationalizing "diversification" as the reason for starting another company for a kid to run—the "run" will often be into the ground. After a season of working for the family business, let the adult children raise the idea of diversification.
- Their first "real job" at the company will not involve direct supervision by another family member.

Owning a family business certainly has financial benefits. One might be the family factor in work compensation. Some families openly pay a family member more than they'd pay a non-family member for the same position. If you go down this track, be open and honest about it. Don't hide or bury the family factor. Hiding it only creates a secret with power greater than you can imagine.

A Track to Run On

Governance and rules will never solve everything. Governance will give you a track to run on and will save you some headaches, particularly by keeping many issues from getting too personal.

Governance, properly developed and utilized, can free you to focus on things like a shared, compelling vision for the future. It can free you to develop a contagious, attractive culture. And it can help you to secure a lasting legacy.

SIXTEEN

the cultural covenant

> Culture is the way we do things around here.
> —Terrence Deal and Allan Kennedy
> (Quoted in Brené Brown, Daring Greatly)

I've never known a culture of one.

The fact is, culture does not exist in isolation, nor is it created in isolation. Therefore, any move toward isolation is a move away from culture. Keep that in mind, particularly if you're a man. Andy Stanley recently said, "As men move through their thirties, forties, and particularly through their fifties, they have a tendency to drift toward isolation, independence and autonomy."[1] He didn't mean it as a compliment.

Be careful here! We are built for relationship, and culture is always created in the context of relationship.

If culture really were the way you did things around your business, as Brené Brown suggested, then what would your employees have to say about your culture? How do you "do things around here"? How would you describe your culture? How can you shape your culture? Or is culture something that "just is"? How can you create the specific kind of culture you want?

What Cultures Do You Admire?

For a moment, think about the kinds of cultures you admire. What do you admire about them? Apply each of your five senses to the issue of culture. What do you admire about a culture's

- appearance?
- sound?
- smell?
- feel?
- taste?

Brené Brown has offered some amazing ideas relative to culture. Throughout her book *The Gifts of Imperfection*, she defined ten "guideposts" for what she called "Wholehearted Living." She described what those who strive to live with their whole hearts, who work at being fully alive, aim to cultivate and what they labor to let go of:

1. Cultivating Authenticity: Letting go of what people think
2. Cultivating Self-Compassion: Letting go of perfectionism
3. Cultivating a Resilient Spirit: Letting go of numbing and powerlessness
4. Cultivating Gratitude and Joy: Letting go of scarcity and fear of the dark

5. Cultivating Intuition and Trusting Faith: Letting go of the need for certainty
6. Cultivating Creativity: Letting go of comparison
7. Cultivating Play and Rest: Letting go of exhaustion as a status symbol and productivity as self-worth
8. Cultivating Calm and Stillness: Letting go of anxiety as a lifestyle
9. Cultivating Meaningful Work: Letting go of self-doubt and "supposed to"
10. Cultivating Laughter, Song and Dance: Letting go of being cool and "always in control"[2]

Does any of this describe the culture you want? What kind of loyal, competent employees might this type of culture attract? What would it be like to create a culture in your organization with a clear bent toward taking action? What if you didn't wait for a crisis?

The Elements of a Cultural Covenant

At a professional continuing education conference several years ago, I heard Caleb Brown and Amy Mullen speak on generational differences in the work force. They also took time to inject some thoughts on culture. They developed a little acronym:

Communication
Understanding
Leadership
Tasks
Unbiased
Responsibility
Energy[3]

All of these might make great tenets for your own Cultural Covenant, but really, they're only a starting place for discussion. You can find other elements, perhaps more relevant to your own situation, in all kinds of places.

One day I was working out at the gym and began visiting with a woman who, along with her husband, owned a successful business and had a long, successful marriage. "We made humor a part of our marriage and our business," she explained. "It relaxes and binds people together." Don't you want to be a part of relationships and cultures full of humor? I do!

How about creativity? Do you want your culture to be creative? How do cultures foster creativity? One way is to "pass the peace pipe" and tell stories around the campfire. When we become good storytellers, amazing ideas emerge. You also can try to grow some creativity in a petri dish. Interesting things grow in petri dishes! We often use them to identify harmful bacteria and virus strains, but petri dishes can also generate positive things.

Let me explain. A son who had been working with his dad in the family business for two or three years one day heard his father ask, "How does a young guy know what he wants to do for the rest of his life?" Had I been the son, I'm not sure how I would have responded. I could have taken offense. But doesn't that kind of question reflect the sort of culture we want in family businesses? One in which both fathers and mothers can ask such questions, and probably more importantly, where the sons and daughters can wrestle with them? That's a petri dish. If we don't create cultures like this, we end up with what Miroslav Volf described in *Against the Tide*: "We live in a smorgasbord culture in which everything is interesting but nothing really matters."[4]

Mother Teresa, once asked how she could give her life to the poor, the homeless, and the sick on the streets of Calcutta, replied that when she looked in their eyes, she saw Jesus. None of us are Mother Teresa, but what sort of cultures might exist in our families and in our businesses if we took a Mother Teresa approach? With family? With employees? With customers? With vendors? With our communities? I daresay we'd work and live on another planet. We would literally change our world.

Take responsibility not only for the culture that now exists in your family or business, but also for the culture you want to create. Andy Stanley said, "Irresponsible behavior shifts the burden to someone else."[5] We *must* take responsibility! As Ghandi once said, "Be the change you want to see."

Creating a Cultural Covenant

We often work with our clients to develop their Cultural Covenant, a living document representing their personalized "Ten Commandments." These give the organization its rules to live by. They are very personal.

One client included a tenet in the company's Cultural Covenant that read, "She's not out to get me." Another one included, "We all want this to succeed." Another great tenet read, "Attribute positive motives"—in other words, believe the best about the other person. Before I even knew what a Cultural Covenant was, I heard this one: "When task isn't working, pull back to relationship." Usually these kinds of statements get forged in the fires of intense relationship, even out of the flames of conflict.

If we really want to make use of the Cultural Covenant, we laminate it when it's ready for prime time. A friend once said, "If it's important, laminate it." I've stolen that statement and passed it on to clients. We're not as likely to lose a laminated piece of paper. You could even consider going a step further—frame it. Put it in a highly visible and prominent spot.

What we focus on, we move toward. When you focus on your Cultural Covenant, your culture will become more like you want it to be.

Building Culture

Let me give you a few suggestions for culture building in your company.

- Try to create a culture that keeps the conversation going. Too many cultures require us to vote. Voting leads to either/or and win/lose. When we discover I'm right and you're wrong (and isn't that true most of the time?), usually the dialogue ends. I want a culture that keeps the dialogue going.
- When relationship isn't working, revisit history. *There was a time when we got along.* What drew you together to get married? To start the business? To dream of clean water? What was it like back when "it" was working?
- Strive to create a culture of intentionality. Live on purpose, with purpose. Clarify your vision, and you will live more purposefully.
- Cultural change happens slowly. Don't get in a hurry! The poet Wendell Berry said, "To be patient in an emergency is a terrible trial."[6]
- Try to create a culture that invites disagreement. No leader, in her heart of hearts, wants to be surrounded by yes men. Respectful disagreement will only enhance

the culture for which you are fighting. We can disagree without being disagreeable.
- Jeff Henderson, in a series of talks titled *Climate Change*, said, "I have a climate that goes with me wherever I go." He suggested that we ask a question of those closest to us: "What's it like to be on the other side of me?" If you want to change your culture, I challenge you to ask this question of the members of your team. "The climate dictates the forecast," Henderson said. "The forecast will remain the same until the climate changes."[7]
- Ask yourself a question: "Does our culture encourage me to become a better person?"
- Make being resilient a value in your organization. Last summer I went mountain biking with a good friend. He had recently heard a TED talk on "grit." As we rode, we discussed the need to be resilient, to be able to bounce back. You can't learn resilience from a book. You can't bounce back unless you've gotten knocked around. Like in handball, the ball bounces back when it encounters something harder (more immovable) than itself. To bounce back, you have to hit a wall.
- Are we going to throw another log on the fire, or are we going to pause and say to ourselves, "Let's think about this"?

I recently began discussing "bedrock truths" with a client. I asked, "What do you know to be true about your partner? When you are apart and you encounter something secondhand that your partner did or said, something that seems to fly in the face of your Cultural Covenant (your bedrock truths), do you give your partner the benefit of the doubt? Or do you fire off an angry email?"

Cling to bedrock truths! And then, when you get back together, have a conversation: "This is what I heard. Did you say this? Is that what you meant? How can we stick together on this? Let's talk about this."

Explore Your Culture of Origin

The moment two people come together in a marriage or in a business partnership, they merge two separate "cultures of origin." When we come together, we each bring our "stuff" to the table. To create the kind of culture that attracts and retains the kinds of people we want to have on our team, and those we want to serve, it is imperative to explore our cultures of origin. We need to understand where we've been and where we need or want to go.

Many marriages have battled long into the night over colliding cultures of origin. Fights about money, parenting, faith, decision-making, and even how to fight often have differing cultures of origin as a root cause. When these cultures merge, therefore, we have to be gentle and slow things down to create forward-moving cultures in which all participants buy in. This is another reason to pursue a Cultural Covenant in your organization.

To get a quick idea of how culture of origin can affect you, think of how decisions were made in your family as you grew up. Did decisions normally reflect the values that guided your family? Could it have been said, for example, "We value transparent communication. Therefore, we will gently approach family members about the hurt we feel when they put us down in front of others"? Or would it have sounded more like, "I'd better not say anything, because she might get mad at me"? Fear will rule decision-making if values don't. And fear is a terrible slumlord.

Culture Trumps Vision

Michael Hyatt writes a popular blog. A few years ago he wrote about attending a convention where he sat on a panel discussing "How to Change Organizational Culture." The panel leader began the session by stating, "Culture trumps vision." Hyatt wrote,

> Leaders often wonder why they can't get traction in making the changes they know are necessary. They articulate a new vision. They change a few policies. They might even replace a few key people. But nothing substantive changes. The problem is that culture is largely invisible to those inside of it. It's like water to a fish or air to a bird. It's simply the environment we live in."[8]

I like to say, "We're all frogs in kettles. It takes a frog living in a kettle other than my own to tell me I'm going to end up boiled." While the heat is being turned up in my cozy little kettle, I remain blissfully unaware of my imminent demise.

I also like to say, "If you live in this town, this is the water you drink."

I once facilitated a team meeting with a client. One administrative staff person, when asked about her job and the culture in which she worked, replied, "Ninety-five percent of the time, I'm happy to come to work. The other 5 percent, I live with." I wish her kind of thinking characterized every person in every organization!

What statements come out of the mouths of your staff members? Listen to them. If they sound like the one I just recounted, you are part of a culture that will attract and retain the kinds of people you want to be around for a long time to come. Culture does indeed trump vision.

The Challenge of Taking Action

I recently spoke to a group about succession planning for family businesses. I titled my talk, "Mediatin,' Navigatin,' and Picture Takin.'" I commented on the challenge family businesses face in taking action for successful succession planning. I observed that most don't take action until some sort of crisis occurs.

Why do you think that is? Some would cite cost. Some might ask, "Well, who can help us with that?" Others will listen to a talk like mine and say, "Yeah, we do need to talk about this stuff," only to go home and jump right back into working *in* the business. Most of us are so busy working *in* the business that we don't take the time to work *on* the business . . . until a crisis occurs. Then we take action, but only because events force us to do so.

Stephen Covey spoke of "Quadrant Two" time management in his book *The 7 Habits of Highly Effective People*. He meant that we need to focus on things that are not *urgent* but are *important*. "Urgent" means putting out fires. "Important" means fire prevention and fire safety.[9] We could all stand to heed Smokey's reminder: "Only you can prevent forest fires!"

So what happens when we wait for a crisis to hit? What happens when we find ourselves in crisis mode? Covey tells us to be proactive rather than reactive. When crisis hits, we typically react. The amygdala, the part of our brain designed to help us survive perilous situations, kicks into gear and we do one of three things: fight, flee, or freeze. None of those reactions gets us where we really want to go.

A thought occurred to me as I gave my talk. If blood started spurting from an artery in my arm, I would react quickly by doing whatever it takes to stop the bleeding. I would not think, "How is this going to affect my arm in five or ten years?" The "whatever it takes" thinking might lead to actions that lead to scars and lack of functionality down the road, after the crisis passes. I might have to use a tourniquet. If I did, the long-term, unintended consequences might include the loss of an arm.

Could the same thing be true when we slip into crisis mode in our family business? "Whatever it takes" overlooks long-term consequences. Haste can, indeed, make waste. When we're in crisis mode, we tend to make on-the-spot decisions we may later regret. These decisions can leave us, and those around us, victims of unintended consequences of the worst kind.

Most of the crises I see in family business tend to be related more to relationship and communication than to business cycles or the economy. These types of crises can lead us to sell at an inopportune moment. They can lead us to fire a key employee who might have become the perfect general manager. They can lead to a rupture in family relationships that might never be repaired.

Don't wait for the crisis! Find a way to get the conversation started. Get some help. Seek out a family business counselor. You'll be glad you did, and so will your family and your business.

A Sample Cultural Covenant

Here's a sample of a Cultural Covenant. Don't copy it. You have to develop your own and then own it. As one client said of his Cultural Covenant, "I look at it every day. It's on my refrigerator and I'm reminded of the things we have agreed upon."

I think he's laminated it . . .

SAMPLE CULTURAL COVENANT

1. Empathy for one another
2. Respect for each other's roles
3. Dedication to common goals
4. Respect for past, present, future
5. Change—how to handle it
6. Communication—listen to understand
7. Education—encourage certification and training to grow personally and as a team
8. Stewardship—land management
9. Economic Diversification—we are committed to it
10. Family—extends beyond blood to employees
11. Check your pride at the door. Be willing to do any job; whatever it takes.

Let's Be Intentional

Recognize that your culture *will* be shaped, whether intentionally or (too often) by default. Let's be part of raising the bar! Let's be intentional about shaping our cultures.

I think of a great line by Andy Stanley: "What gets rewarded gets repeated."[10] How can you reward what you want to see repeated in your family business?

- part five -

STAY ENGAGED

WORK, MONITOR, AND EVOLVE
"THE PLAN" AS TOGETHER
WE DARE GREATLY

SEVENTEEN

▼

changing roles

I joined my business partner more than twenty years ago. I came as an employee at age thirty-eight with a good bit of life experience as well as a fair amount of business experience. And yet, little did I know the journey I had just embarked upon.

My partner founded our company. When I joined him, he'd already been in business in our town for nearly twenty-five years, so I encountered a certain amount of "this is the way we do things around here." Still, he graciously allowed me to set the course for myself and eventually for our company. His "this is the way we do things around here" became more of "this is the way I've done things and will continue to do things." He let go of me, in a sense, but not necessarily of his history.

I have to say, most founders aren't as liberal as he has been with me. I am very grateful.

Fast-forward to 2013. We had been equal partners for many years, and I felt an increasing storehouse of resentment growing within me. Much of it came from my belief that I had been "out-producing" my partner for many years and was being short-changed financially, even though for four to five years I had been receiving some extra compensation as a "guaranteed payment."

I admit that I had a hard time having direct conversations about the issue with my partner. When I finally expressed how I felt and what *I* had decided would be fair, my partner replied that it seemed a bit unfair to him that I hadn't told him any of this earlier. He was right.

When I suggested that I would compensate him in the form of a buyout, the idea ran counter to how he'd envisioned the future. Had he known my true feelings earlier, maybe we'd have changed things earlier. We didn't, and we proceeded with my plan for transition.

Through all of this, my business partner and I remained "married." I made a commitment long ago that I wouldn't leave him, contrary to the many people who had left him. I wanted to prove that not everyone leaves. When you make that kind of commitment, you "put up" with certain things. Maybe I put up with too much over time. But we are still together and I think that counts for something, not only for us, but also for our staff, our families, and our community.

At the end of 2013, we had some bills to pay and some bonuses to give out. In the past, when he and I were 50/50 partners, I considered myself the generous one and so often would advocate for larger bonuses. I learned some things along the way from my partner about holding off. All of a sudden, now that he was a minority owner, it felt like all of these payments were coming out of *my* pocket. Before, fifty cents of every dollar we "spent" on bonuses wasn't mine. Not so now. All of a sudden, I realized that I was not as generous as I once thought I was.

In this new role as majority owner, I understand the "founder" role a whole lot better. I see with greater insight the things my partner dealt with all those years. I'm more understanding of what he went through. Can we truly understand "the other" without this type of role reversal? What is it, really, to walk in someone else's moccasins? I will never know what it was like to start *this* business. We have morphed and in a sense started several businesses since we began our partnership, but I don't know what those early days were like. I do, however, know some of what it is to be the majority owner, to be the one who calls the shots. I feel as if my leadership has blossomed. I've rediscovered an imaginative, "what if?" approach that I believe can help our company, our clients, and our community.

I also believe it's easier for a follower (owner) than it is for a founder (owner) to move to a more flattened hierarchy when it comes to governing a business. And I think it's easier to let go if you are a follower rather than a founder. Just as parents have a hard time letting go of children and encouraging them to leave the nest, so I believe it's hard for a founder to let "his child" leave the nest. After all, the founder, like the parent, "birthed" this child and raised it. Surely this innocent, helpless thing cannot possibly survive on its own!

Who started *your* company? Did you or someone else get the ball rolling? Your answers will give valuable insight to you, your family, your team, and your advisors when you want to gain understanding about how you relate to others.

When Things Don't Go as Planned

I've observed many founders' attempts at transition and have noted how difficult it can be to deal with things that don't go as planned.

Often the founder, particularly when the organization fits a hierarchical model, simply throws more hours at the problem to try and fix it. That often works—and that's the problem.

The next generation may not *want* to throw more hours at it. Its members came into the business with the idea of balancing life and work. So it's a real problem if the founder expects them, if they are *really* committed, to throw more hours at some challenge. If we don't define what we mean by "fix" it, we will watch generations clash before our very eyes.

For a moment I want to revisit Pogo: "We've met the enemy, and he is us!" Just for a second, let's drop the plural and make it, "I've met the enemy, and he is me!"

What paralysis comes from your fears? Many times, the obstacle that weighs most heavily in overcoming inertia is the current majority owner. How do I get out of the way? Sometimes it helps to physically get out of the way for an extended period of time.

Late in the summer of 2013, my wife, daughter, and I went to Europe for five weeks. I have to confess that I didn't really do anything for our twenty-fifth anniversary. Nor did I do much for my wife's fiftieth birthday; and that June, my daughter graduated from college. So I considered this trip a bit of a makeup.

We had a great time hiking, visiting friends, and being restored and renewed. But one positive, unintended consequence also happened. Our next-gen guy at the business, who had been with us barely two years, took some huge initiative in my absence. He had a goal of not calling me. He also made it a point to meet with as many of our financial planning and asset management clients as possible.

The proof of the value of all of this came upon my return. I stopped by the office for a minute the day we flew home and found him visiting with a client I'd worked with for nearly fifteen years. I gave the client a piece of chocolate and said hi, but the client seemed totally engaged with our next-gen guy. At first I thought, "Hey, I'm the primary advisor here!" But upon reflection, I thought, "This is exactly what we've been planning for." That's an unintended consequence of a positive kind. And I don't know if it would have happened had I not left the office for five weeks. I really doubt it would have. The initiative shown by our young associate, combined with my time away, accelerated my transition and allowed me to focus on Family Business Counsel.

Some elders are like the young-ish business owner I heard about this week. An associate of his said this guy lives as he does because he thinks he's had some sort of premonition that he'll be dead by age fifty. He has only five or six years left. So in some ways, he's wiser than most of us; he recognizes his own mortality. But here's the paradox: He lives and works as though he's going to live forever. He pushes it to the limit and beyond. If something did happen to him, I doubt his business or his family would be ready for him to go. He lives as though he's invincible and immortal.

Elders beware . . .

Stages of Decline

Jim Collins, author of *Good to Great* and *Built to Last*, more recently authored a book titled *How the Mighty Fall*. In it, he describes the fall of some heavyweight companies. We would all do well to listen to Collins and his team's research as they describe what they call the "Stages of Decline."

> Stage 1: Hubris Born of Success
> Stage 2: Undisciplined Pursuit of More

Stage 3: Denial of Risk and Peril
Stage 4: Grasping for Salvation
Stage 5: Capitulation to Irrelevance or Death[1]

In describing Stage 4, Collins says that "common saviors" include:

- a charismatic, visionary leader,
- a bold but untested strategy,
- a radical transformation,
- a dramatic cultural revolution,
- a hoped-for blockbuster product,
- a "game changing" acquisition.[2]

Collins insists that there is a way to turn things around in Stage 4, *if* we practice "recovery and renewal." *Recovery* sounds like a word for addicts, while *renewal* connotes something new that needs to happen. Neither of those things comes naturally to the founder or the entrepreneur as they move to the elder stage. Nevertheless, these "unnatural" things are at the heart of what it means to be a wise elder.

Collins says this renewal and recovery can happen if we don't lose hope, because "when you abandon hope, you should begin preparing for the end."[3] I would add that this hope must be well grounded and anchored.

What Do They Want?

What does the next-gen leader want of the elder? I would say two things: first, to not feel like she always has to look over her shoulder for the elder's approval; and second, to have a resource to go to when times get tough or when she faces a difficult decision.

And what does the elder want? First, to not be thought of as "in the way." And second, to have someone knocking on his door every so often, asking for a piece of advice or a listening ear.

Don't both the next-gen leader and the elder really want the same thing? I think they do, but neither tends to clearly articulate to the other what they want.

It's easy to pigeonhole people based on who they've been. Do you want people doing that with you? I don't. I want people believing in the person I am becoming. Assume the best about people, not the worst, and watch what they become. Your shy, introverted daughter might one day spread her wings and soar. But if you can't get over seeing her as a snotty-nosed kid, can she ever become the CEO?

My partner is seventeen years older than I am. He's been working on his transition for quite a while. A big transition occurred while I was away the summer of 2013. He moved out of his office. We remodeled it, and I moved in. The move allowed me to meet with clients and not utilize the conference room as much.

It certainly was easier for me to move in than it was for our founder to move out. One of the challenges he faced was all the stuff he'd accumulated over forty-plus years being in that office. He isn't necessarily a hoarder, but he admits he has a hard time throwing things away. Just this week, he voiced one of the reasons that he finds it hard to throw things away. "Somebody might be able to make use of this stuff," he explained. And if it cost money to acquire it, he reasoned, then it sort of dishonors the effort and money spent acquiring it if you simply discard it.

Having said all of that, he's making great headway. He's come to realize that what he values, others may not.

Don't we all know that if we keeled over tomorrow, much of the stuff we value would get quickly discarded? That might be books. It might be photos or furniture. It might even be business systems we've spent years building. Thinking through these things might help me carry my stuff with a little bit looser grip . . . I hope. So I've told my partner, "Show me how to do this transition thing. I'm not that far behind you." I know he wants to do it well. I want him to do it well too.

Many law firms have policies to let the old guys and gals keep an office. They give them the title "ex officio" or "emeritus," something like the retired professor who still teaches one class a year.

Very few family businesses have this kind of place for the elder. But what if that changed? The know-how and the know-who of elders become most valuable in their later years. So why not utilize it? Too often the elder fears hearing, "It's time." Or they feel as though they're being edged out or put out to pasture.

I believe we need to separate productive from valuable. No doubt, certain capacities decline as we age. Productivity can be one of those things if we measure it in terms of energy or even sales. But value? Come on! How valuable is the wisdom and perspective of an elder? They've weathered business, market, and even relational cycles, over and over. And how valuable are the relationships they've nurtured over the years? Mine them!

A further word to the sage elder when considering your next-gen guy: You want him to soar, so don't clip his wings. If he should fall flat, let him do that on his own and not because you made it impossible for him to take flight.

On Becoming Grumpy

Every family business should answer the purpose question: Why do we do what we do? Or, why does this company exist? One client answered the question by saying, "To make money."

As we discussed the question with both his team and the next-gen group, we decided that the founder's why worked for him, but the next-gen group must come up with its own why. Yes, the founder's why got the group this far, but it wouldn't get it where the next-gen folks want to go. They have to discover their own why. This will be a sea change for the company.

Along the way, we've begun to ask if making money is really the founder's why. It's been fun to explore this and watch the "transitioning of the why." We're wondering if making money is the validator rather than the motivator for the founder. While a motivator is what gets you up in the morning, a validator is more a way of keeping score.

If the founder is not gracious about his why morphing into a next-gen why, he can get grumpy, only to validate the truth that grumpy old men live.

The one thing my wife can say to me that really gets me is, "You're like your dad." Don't we all grow up saying we'll never be like our parents? And then sometime, maybe around age forty-five or fifty, we go, "Uh-oh. I'm becoming just like my dad." Mannerisms, phrases, even looks start to resemble our parents.

My dad has been gone for sixteen years. I can recount many times when I acted in a disrespectful way toward him. These past eight or ten years, my respect for him has increased exponentially. Maybe "respect your elders" isn't such a bad idea after all.

At age fifty-nine, I'm not sure I can quite yet be considered an "elder," though in the view of the thirtysomethings in our company, I'm sure I am. It's all about perspective, right? Remember *Grumpy Old Men*, the movie with Walter Matthau and Jack Lemmon? Well, it's true. Old men *can* get grumpy . . . and I count myself as a candidate for entering the land of the grumpy.

When I returned from our 2013 trip to Europe, I realized that I could quickly get back into the rat race. So I began to think about a daily, weekly, monthly, quarterly, and annual rhythm. What would be healthy? We were just converting to a new calendar system, and I asked my "right arm" in our office to help me build a calendar with the right rhythm. She did.

Quickly I began to fudge. I scheduled more appointments than I should have. I soon realized that interruptions are going to happen. If I stick to the ideal calendar, however, I will have room for interruptions. When I violate that rhythm, the interruptions will give me no breathing room and I'll resent them. Although we all know how interruptions can sometimes be the coolest things, if I resent them, it's highly unlikely I will see the "cool" in them. My light-bulb moment came when I realized that if I don't respect the rhythm of my ideal calendar, my violations give me no breathing room. When I have no breathing room, I get grumpy, and others pay for it. John Ortberg wrote a book titled *The Me I Want to Be*. "Grumpy" is not the me I want to be.

For me, this is elder stuff. Here I was in 2013, fifty-seven years old, and only then figuring out "grumpy." Maybe you learned this stuff early on. It's taken me awhile. I will still get grumpy, but, as I aspire to be a good elder, I hope Grumpy will take his place as a dwarf on my shelf and no longer act like the Jolly Green Giant.

EIGHTEEN

▼

the photo album

Do you keep photo albums? If you do, what kind of photos do you consider album worthy? When do you take photos for them? When you visit landmarks, experience significant events, and spend time with special people, right?

A fat business "photo album" can be a great indicator for me of progress along this journey toward health in a family business, as well as an indicator of the team's engagement.

As you travel as a family business, look for landmarks (significant achievements—Dad starts consistently using "we" instead of "I" statements in public about the family business), events ("We were away for a month and the kids actually got along better and worked together better than when we're around."), and people ("Joe has changed. In the past when things didn't go his way, he would take his ball and go home. Now he's consistently staying engaged.").

Take a Look... or Two

How often do you look at your wedding album? Do you ever? If you're like me, I'll bet you do. What does it do for you? It reminds me of the early days. It reminds me of why I got married in the first place. It reminds me of how far we've come in almost thirty years.

Photo albums aren't just places to store old photos. We need to break them out from time to time to remind us of what's important.

Breaking out the business photo album can do a number of things. One of the main things we get from looking at it is to remember things such as:

- Why did we start this business?
- Times were tough then, but it was worth it.
- Look how far we've come!
- In rough times, I can come back to the photo album and find new courage to carry on.

Celebrations should also make their way into the photo album. Take time to celebrate! Celebrate the wins. And as you celebrate, take pictures—snapshots to put in your photo album.

While we need to take photos from the start (think of a baby book for the business), it's a sign of a healthy culture when you see photos regularly added to the photo album through the years and families sitting around looking at it.

Am I talking here about literal pictures in a literal album? Maybe. But even if they're not literal photos, you must find *some* way to recognize, collect, and review the landmarks, events, and people that have made, make, and will make up the fabric of your family business.

It's an Honor

How do you react when you see a picture of yourself? You might say, "We were young then," or, "I can't believe that shirt!" But one thing I'll bet money on: if you see yourself in another person's photo album, it warms your heart. You feel honored.

The same thing is true with the photo album of the family business. You honor your people by taking their picture.

In our digital age, it's okay to throw a video or two into your photo album. One client speaks of people about to retire taking a victory lap. A victory lap might be a project they get to run the last year they work. It's something that has "them" stamped all over it. *Take videos of victory laps.*

We run into substance abuse in many families we counsel. One comes to mind where alcohol has created a lot of problems and has even produced serious liability issues for the business. Over time, the younger generation has said, "We want to change the attitude toward alcohol in our community." That's a photo op! Family businesses can change communities! They can change cultures!

As a family business counselor, I aspire to practice what I preach. But we're all human, so my success rate is somewhere south of 100 percent. Yours probably is too. But keep at it!

My Cloudy Day Reading File

I have my own photo album. I call it my "Cloudy Day Reading File." In it are emails like the one I received today from a next-gen team member:

> Good Morning Mark,
>
> I just wanted to write you a quick email wishing you a Merry Christmas and Happy New Year.
>
> I also want to personally thank you for all that you've done for our family this past year. In the short time that we've been working with you, I have seen some sort of positive change in EVERY person within our family. It is truly safe to say that this is thanks to your patience, insight and thoughtfulness concerning the issues that we face as not only a business, but more importantly as a family. Without it I fear that we would still be continuing through the wilderness without any hope of getting to the promised land.
>
> So from the bottom of my heart, thank you. And Merry Christmas from my family to you and yours.

I have to pull out my Cloudy Day Reading File from time to time. It reminds me that this is all worth it. It reminds me of why I do what I do.

Why not let yours do the same thing for you?

NINETEEN

▼

legacy

> Let us have ambition enough to keep our simplicity,
> our frugality and our integrity, and transmit these virtues
> as the fairest of inheritance to our children.
>
> —John Adams
> (Said to his wife, Abigail, after being in Paris and away
> from family, having been exposed to the "good life.")

What legacy do you want to leave behind? Is it wealth? Is it the business? Is it your view of work?

Not long ago, I read a book by Miroslav Volf called *The End of Memory*, a meditation on forgiveness and reconciliation. Volf is Croatian, and he grew up in the former Yugoslavia under Tito's regime.

Volf described his time in the Yugoslavian military in the 1980s. He'd been interrogated, beyond what was reasonable, by a soldier he called Captain G. Years later he tried in a variety of ways, unsuccessfully, to track down Captain G. After coming up empty, he "staged" (in his imagination) an encounter with Captain G.

He first attempted a South African Truth and Reconciliation Commission–type setting, complete with Desmond Tutu presiding. Captain G didn't admit to much.

Volf next attempted the meeting in a bar, one-on-one. Again, Captain G didn't give him what he wanted; he tried to make excuses and also pointed out Volf's own shortcomings. Volf ended up getting angry and walking out.

In the end, Volf realized that for this exercise to benefit anyone, all involved needed a third party, and not just any third party—a therapist wouldn't suffice. They needed someone who could mediate, who could bring care to both, who wanted a good future for both, and who could bring hope to both.

Volf imagined that third party as God.[1]

Now, I'm not God, but is it possible to imagine that kind of facilitation in a family business? We all need some sort of relational reconciliation. The work isn't restricted to the worst of the worst. We all have "issues" with others that require some humble work. We all could use a "God-like" facilitator.

I've discovered that even though I do this kind of work professionally, I can't do it for my own stuff. My wife and I have gone through seasons with several marriage therapists. We both want better for ourselves as a couple. We want to be caught up in a mutually compelling vision for the future. We now have a financial advisor who helps us align our money with what we see as a healthy vision for the future, one we share.

The Crucial Place of Forgiveness

This past fall I participated in a daylong panel focused on succession planning. We handed out three-by-five cards before lunch for people to write their questions. We spent the afternoon session responding to those questions.

I handled one question that asked, "What do I do when I can't get along with a family member?" I took a deep breath and replied, "You have to decide how important the value of forgiveness is in your family. Forgiveness can be extended unilaterally. For forgiveness to be complete, I need to forgive as many times as it takes until the offense no longer separates the relationship." I paused and then continued. "But, for true *reconciliation* to take place," I said, "it takes two. I must feel your arms around me. You must feel my arms around you."

I've watched many families *not* pursue reconciliation. It often becomes a Hatfield and McCoy family feud. Particularly when land is involved, I've seen families divide. They usually end up splitting the property in two.

In reflecting on this reality, I pictured a piece of paper being torn in two, again and again and again. Pretty soon, what do you end up with? Scraps. Pieces. Nothing of value. That can happen with family land, generation after generation after generation.

I recalled the repeated Old Testament warning that God would visit "the iniquity of the fathers upon the children unto the third and fourth generation."[2] While I don't understand that concept completely, I think I've seen it happen.

I have a client who is trying to beat the 3 percent statistic. The business is trying to make it to the fourth generation. One part of the family wants to split the business, but the fourth generation wants to stick together. They are standing up and saying, "This s*#% stops here!"

What inheritance do you want to pass on? Families spend so much time working on how to pass along wealth and business to the next generation. What about passing on a legacy of forgiveness and reconciliation?

I've been privileged to facilitate family meetings where Mom and Dad share not only their finances, but also their life stories and what matters to them. After one of those meetings, I took Dad aside and said, "Do you know what kind of an inheritance you just gave your kids? Most families hear this message from someone else, in other people's words, after you're gone. Your kids heard your words from your own mouth while you're still here. What an inheritance!"

And I say, what a legacy!

Beware Residual Resentment

Brené Brown wrote her book *Daring Greatly* based on Teddy Roosevelt's speech "The Man in the Arena."[3] I highly recommend her work (no doubt you've noticed the many times I've quoted her). She did a TED talk on vulnerability that went viral. In it, she said, "People who have a strong sense of love and belonging believe they are worthy of love and belonging. That's it. . . . They are wholehearted people." She went on to describe the traits she discovered these people have in common. They all have:

- *courage* to be imperfect,
- *compassion* to be kind to themselves first and then to others,
- *connection* as a result of authenticity, and
- they fully embraced *vulnerability*.[4]

When we're not putting these things into practice, we need to be careful of passing on what I call residual resentment. And what do I mean by residual resentment?

Suppose you get in a car wreck. Your car isn't totaled, but the windshield gets bashed in. You do your best to clean up all of the glass in the car. A month later, on a hot summer day, you get in your car wearing flip-flops. All of a sudden, you feel a sharp pain in the bottom of your foot. You realize you have a shard of glass in your foot.

That is residual resentment.

The pain caused by the glass shard motivates you to take it out as quickly as you can. And what if you don't? Over time, the jagged glass becomes embedded in your foot and infection sets in.

Residual resentment can be even worse. Unaddressed, it can become contagious in your family. Is that part of the legacy you want to pass on? I doubt it.

Residual resentment expresses itself in statements like, "Dad always liked you better," or, "He's always gotten away with murder around here." Oftentimes it is based only on misperception. Left untreated, infection sets in.

Don't let the infection and the contagious nature of residual resentment contaminate your family business! And by all means, don't make it part of your inheritance to your kids and grandkids.

It's Not Too Late

I firmly believe that reconciliation is possible, so long as we draw breath. I watched this happen in my own family.

My sister and Dad had a strained relationship. I don't know all the reasons, but I had the great privilege of observing something significant near the end of Dad's days when he lay in St. Charles Medical Center in Bend, Oregon. We knew he didn't have long, and so my sister, who lived in Southern California, flew up to be with him. As Dad's blood pressure dipped dangerously low and he began fading, he asked me from time to time, "Will she be here soon?" or, "How soon will she get here?"

My wife picked up my sister at the Portland airport and drove her to Bend. When my dad knew they were getting close, he rallied. After my sister arrived, I witnessed a moment of forgiveness and reconciliation that I will never forget. I consider it holy ground!

It's *not* too late for reconciliation.

As I write, I realize that my dad passed on to me a legacy of reconciliation and forgiveness. Isn't it interesting that this is where I get to spend my best efforts with my best hours? I help families face difficult, crucial conversations, engaged and daring greatly, and along the way, I watch them pursue forgiveness and reconciliation. For that, I am forever grateful.

I want to be a wholehearted person! I hope you do, too, and that this wholeheartedness is part of the inheritance and legacy you intend to pass on to subsequent generations.

So dare greatly! Stay engaged in the journey! And Godspeed.

acknowledgments

No one likes reading acknowledgments . . . unless they read their name. So, I'll be brief and hope I don't forget anyone.

The idea for this book began a little more than three years ago, as my wife and I were planning for an extended time away. She encouraged me to build in some writing time. So, Lyn, thank you for putting up with me then and over these past three years. As we've just passed the thirty-year marker in marriage, I (and it's not just Facebook posts that say it) married up!

For a while after that trip, I tried to carve out time to write monthly. That was a challenge. Maybe that's why this project didn't get done earlier. Having said that, the time that has elapsed has allowed for the gathering of more stories. To Family Business Counsel clients, current, past, and future, I am grateful that you let me continue to eavesdrop on the stories being written in the lives of your families and your businesses. And thanks to all the other families and businesses I've gotten to meet along the way who are not clients but who nonetheless enrich my life and the story I'm now getting to tell.

I could not be more grateful to my coworkers. From the beginning: Dan Corrigan, for the never-ending support and encouragement; Jan Jackson, who defines loyalty; Maria Olsen, who was my right arm and more; Tommy Paterson, who has stepped up in such a big way—to watch you grow is a privilege; Caitlin Sticka, who brightens our office daily and has shown us what it is to fight a good fight, and now Martha Nicol, who is truly running the show at Family Business Counsel. Thank you individually and collectively!

Steve Halliday, you took a really rough piece of stone, a one-hundred-page manuscript, and chiseled it into something I'm proud of. I hope you are too. Darcie Clemen, copy editor and *so much more*—when I raised the white flag, you were there! These two stooped to my novice-ness as an author when they've dealt with names you'd all recognize. Thank you!

This may not count as a village, but it has been a team effort. I'm grateful in more ways than each of you know.

Mark Wickman
McMinnville, Oregon
August 2016

notes

INTRODUCTION
1. "Facts and Figures," Family Business Alliance, http://www.fbagr.org/index.php?option=com_content&view=article&id=117&Itemid=75.

CHAPTER ONE
1. Chris Lowney, *Heroic Leadership* (Chicago: Loyola Press, 2010), 8–9.
2. Anthony de Mello, *Awareness* (New York: Image Books, 1990), 104.
3. Clayton M. Christensen, *The Innovator's Dilemma* (Boston: Harvard Business School Press, 1997), 165.
4. "Watch: Pete Carroll's full interview with Matt Lauer," Today.com, February 5, 2015, http://www.today.com/video/today/56934537#56934537.

CHAPTER TWO
1. Warren Berger, *A More Beautiful Question* (New York: Bloomsbury, 2014), 4.
2. Ibid., 40.
3. Pink discusses this idea in *To Sell Is Human* (New York: Riverhead Books, 2012).
4. Johnny Kaufman, "'Don't Be Afraid of Silence': Interview Tips From NPR Host Rachel Martin," npr.org, November 27, 2013, http://www.npr.org/sections/npr-extra/2013/11/20/246336891/it-s-not-about-you-listening-tips-from-weekend-edition-sunday-host-rachel-martin.
5. Berger, 34–35.

CHAPTER THREE
1. Jeremy Statton, "Why You Might Want to Stop Avoiding Conflict," *Living Better Stories* (blog), August 16, 2013, http://www.jeremystatton.com/avoid-conflict.
2. Andy Stanley, "Common Cause," sermon, North Point Community Church, August 25, 2012, video, 41:02, http://northpoint.org/messages/future-family/common-cause/.
3. Dick Clark, quoted by Jim Collins in *How the Mighty Fall* (New York: Collins Business Essentials, 2009), 116.

4. William Bridges, *The Way of Transition* (New York: Perseus Publishing, 2001), 96.
5. "Book Discussion on *Holding Her Head High*," C-Span.org, March 19, 2008, video, 39:49, http://www.c-span.org/video/?204441-1/janine-turner-holding-head-high.
6. Ibid.
7. Desmond Tutu, *No Future Without Forgiveness* (New York: Doubleday, 2000), 272.
8. The parable is found in Matthew 20:1–16.
9. Gerald May, *The Dark Night of the Soul* (San Francisco: HarperOne, 2005), 81.

CHAPTER FOUR
1. Susan Sokol Blosser, *Letting Go* (Susan Sokol Blosser, 2015), Kindle edition.
2. Denise Kenyon-Rouvinez and John L. Ward, *Family Business Key Issues* (New York: Palgrave Macmillan, 2005), 71.
3. Jason Katims and Gina Fatore, "You've Got Mold," *Parenthood*, season 5, episode 14, directed by Ken Whittingham, 42 min., netflix.com.

CHAPTER FIVE
1. Daniel Pink, "Drive: The surprising truth about what motivates us" (lecture, Royal Society for the encouragement of Arts, Manufactures and Commerce, London, March 10, 2010), https://www.thersa.org/globalassets/pdfs/blogs/rsa-lecture-dan-pink-transcript.pdf, 4.
2. Genesis 29:20 ESV. Taken from the ESV® Bible (The Holy Bible, English Standard Version®), copyright © 2001 by Crossway, a publishing ministry of Good News Publishers. Used by permission. All rights reserved.
3. Genesis 31:43 NLT. Taken from the Holy Bible, New Living Translation. © 1996, 2004, 2007, 2013 by Tyndale House Foundation. Used by permission of Tyndale House Publishers, Inc., Carol Stream, Illinois 60188. All rights reserved.

CHAPTER SIX
1. John Ortberg, *The Me I Want to Be* (Grand Rapids, MI: Zondervan, 2010), 232–34.
2. Matthew 25:24, 25 NIV. Taken from the Holy Bible, New International Version®, NIV®. Copyright © 1973, 1978, 1984, 2011 by Biblica, Inc.™ Used by permission of Zondervan. All rights reserved.
3. Schematic taken from Tagiuri and Davis, found at: http://johndavis.com/three-circle-model-of-the-family-business-system/.

CHAPTER SEVEN
1. Stephen M. R. Covey, *The Speed of Trust* (New York: Free Press, 2005), 59–60.
2. Ibid., 127–222.
3. Andy Crouch, *Playing God: Redeeming the Gift of Power* (Downers Grove, IL: InterVarsity Press, 2013), 147.
4. Luke Naismith, "The A-Frame of Trust," *Knowledge Futures* (blog), May 20, 2007, https://knowledgefutures.wordpress.com/2007/05/20/the-a-frame-of-trust/.
5. Brené Brown, *Rising Strong* (New York: Spiegel & Grau, 2015), 198.
6. Henry Cloud, *Integrity* (New York: Harper Business, 2009), 200.

CHAPTER NINE
1. Michael Gerber, *The E-Myth Revisited* (New York: HarperCollins, 1995), 40.
2. Patrick Lencioni, *Death by Meeting* (San Francisco: Jossey-Bass, 2004).

CHAPTER ELEVEN
1. "Brené Brown on Empathy," YouTube video, 2:53, posted by The RSA, December 10, 2013, https://www.youtube.com/watch?v=1Evwgu369Jw.
2. Stephen Covey, *The 7 Habits of Highly Successful People* (New York: Simon & Schuster, 1989), 239.
3. Daniel Kahneman, *Thinking, Fast and Slow* (New York: Farrar, Straus and Giroux, 2011), 24.
4. Donald Miller, Twitter post, 3:00 p.m., November 16, 2015, https://twitter.com/donaldmiller.
5. Brené Brown, *Daring Greatly* (New York: Penguin, 2012), 15, 184, 192.
6. Covey addresses this idea in *The Speed of Trust* (New York: Free Press, 2006).

CHAPTER TWELVE
1. William Bridges, *Transitions* (New York: Da Capo Press, 2004), 11.
2. William Bridges, "Getting Them Through the Wilderness," wmbridges.com, 1987, http://www.wmbridges.com/pdf/getting-thru-wilderness-2006-v2.pdf.
3. Coco Chanel, quoted in William Bridges, *The Way of Transition* (New York: Perseus Publishing, 2001), 85.
4. Ibid., 130.
5. The story of Rehoboam and the ancient Israelite civil war is in 1 Kings 12.
6. James E. Hughes Jr., *Family: The Compact Among Generations* (New York: Bloomberg Press, 2007), 178–79.

7. Ibid., 181.
8. A friend of mine, in a board meeting, repeated this quote by Rick McKinley.

CHAPTER THIRTEEN
1. Lapin shared this story at a Financial Planning Association (FPA) luncheon I attended in Portland, OR.
2. Viktor Frankl, *Man's Search for Meaning* (New York: Pocket Books, 1959), 65–66.

CHAPTER FOURTEEN
1. Henry Cloud, *Integrity* (New York: Harper Business, 2009), 24, 175.
2. Ibid., 35.
3. Ibid., 53.
4. Jim Collins, *Good to Great* (New York: Harper Business, 2001), 21.

CHAPTER FIFTEEN
1. Denise Kenyon-Rouvinez and John Ward, *Family Business Key Issues* (New York: Palgrave Macmillan, 2005), 44.
2. Ibid. This idea is discussed in chapter 4.
3. Ibid., 63, 70.
4. Ibid., 65.

CHAPTER SIXTEEN
1. Andy Stanley, "Accessible," sermon, North Point Community Church, August 9, 2014, http://northpoint.org/messages/accessible/.
2. Brené Brown, *The Gifts of Imperfection* (Center City, MN: Hazelden, 2010), vii–viii.
3. Caleb Brown and Amy Mullen, Financial Planning Association of Oregon Mid-Winter Conference, February 7, 2012.
4. Miroslav Volf, *Against the Tide* (Grand Rapids, MI: Wm. B. Eerdmans, 2010), 141.
5. Andy Stanley, "The Disproportionate Life," sermon, Preaching Today, September 2011, http://www.preachingtoday.com/sermons/sermons/2011/september/disproportionate.html.
6. Wendell Berry, "Wendell Berry: Poet and Prophet," interview with Bill Moyers, Vimeo, 56:46, October 4, 2013, https://vimeo.com/76122933.
7. Jeff Henderson, "Storm Clouds," *Climate Change* sermon series, part 2, mp3, North Point Church, http://store.northpoint.org/climate-change-part-2.html.
8. Michael Hyatt, "How do you change organizational culture?" blog post, February 22, 2012, http://michaelhyatt.com/changing-organizational-culture.html.

9. Stephen Covey, *The 7 Habits of Highly Effective People* (New York: Simon & Schuster, 2004), 150.
10. Andy Stanley, "Article: Andy Stanley," Catalyst, https://catalystconference.com/read/article-andy-stanley/.

CHAPTER SEVENTEEN
1. Jim Collins, *How the Mighty Fall* (New York: HarperCollins, 2011), 20.
2. Ibid., 22.
3. Ibid., 107.

CHAPTER NINETEEN
1. Miroslav Volf, *The End of Memory* (Grand Rapids, MI: Wm. B. Eerdmans, 2006), 216–26.
2. See Exodus 20:5; Numbers 14:18; Deuteronomy 5:9.
3. Brené Brown, *Daring Greatly* (New York: Penguin, 2012), 1.
4. Brené Brown, "The Power of Vulnerability," 20:19, TED talk video, January 2010, http://www.ted.com/talks/brene_brown_on_vulnerability?language=en.

Made in the USA
San Bernardino, CA
15 January 2020